one man
one car
one tyre

BRIDGESTONE
ULTIMATE PERFORMANCE

PHOTOGRAPHIC CREDIT - grands prix section

Thierry Gromik: 18-19, 64-65, 82-83, 82(3), 83(1), 85(2), 86-87, 88(1), 89, 93(1, 2), 102(2, 3), 111(3, 4), 104-105, 106(1), 110(2), 112-113, 114(1), 118(1), 119(2, 3), 122(1), 126(3), 127, 130(2, 3), 134(1), 135, 136(1), 140(1, 2), 144(1), 145(3), 148(2, 3), 152(1), 153(1), 158-159, 160(3), 161(4), 162(1, 2, 3), 164-165, 166(1, 2), 170(2, 3), 174(1), 175(4), 176(1), 180(1), 181(2), 182-183, 184(2), 186-187, 188(1, 2), 189(3, 4), 190-191, 192(2, 3), 200-201, 204-205, 210, 211(2).
Daniel Reinhard: 80-81, 82(1), 83(2), 85(1, 3), 90-91, 103(2), 106(2, 3), 108-109, 110(1), 114(2, 3), 119(1), 122(2, 3), 124-125, 126(1, 2), 130(1), 134(2), 136(2, 3), 137(3), 140(3), 145(2), 152(2), 156(1, 3), 160(1, 2), 161(1), 162(4), 166(3, 4), 167(3), 170(4), 174(3), 175(1), 176(2, 3), 181(1), 184(1), 194-195, 197(3), 202, 203(1), 206(1), 211(3), 214(1).
Steve Domenjoz: 84(2), 88(3, 4), 92-93, 96-97, 106(4), 114(4), 118(2), 120-121, 132-133, 137(1), 140(4), 142-143, 144(2), 146-147, 148(1), 152(2, 3), 154-155, 161(2, 3), 170(1, 5), 174(2), 180(3), 181(3), 184(3), 188(3), 189(1), 192(1), 196, 197(2), 198(1), 203(2), 206(2), 208-209, 211(1), 212-213, 214(2, 3).
Allsport Management SA: 110(3), 150-151, 161(2), 167(2), 206(2), 192(1).
Masakazu Miyata: 84(3), 111(1), 137(2), 138-139, 144(3), 172-173, 175(2, 3), 189(2).
Jean-Marc Loubat: 78-79, 103(1, 3), 111(2), 145(1), 152(3), 156(2), 167(1, 4), 178-179, 180(2), 197(1), 198(2, 3).
Jean-Marc Lisse: 42-43, 84(1), 100-101, 102(1), 116-117, 128-129, 168-169.

Contents

The players

Eleven teams, twenty two racing drivers. A few engineers, a lot of mechanics and several bosses. Nationalities from Argentina to India, via Japan and Australia, all sharing the same burning love for their job. Formula 1 is a passion and these men, from first to last, all have it in abundance.

McLaren-Mercedes

1. Mika HÄKKINEN

DRIVER PROFILE

- Name : *HÄKKINEN*
- First names : *Mika Pauli*
- Nationality : *Finnish*
- Date of birth : *September 28, 1968*
- Place of birth : *Helsinki (FIN)*
- Lives in : *Monte Carlo (Monaco)*
- Marital status : *married to Erja*
- Kids : *-*
- Hobbies : *badminton, skiing, tennis*
- Favourite music : *Mick Jagger, pop*
- Favourite meal : *finnish food*
- Boissons favorites : *water, Coca-cola*
- Height : *179 cm*
- Weight : *70,5 kg*

STATISTICS | PRIOR TO F1

• Nber of Grand Prix :	145	1987 : *Champion F. Ford*
• Victories :	18	1988 : *Opel Lotus*
• Pole-positions :	26	*Euroseries*
• Best laps :	22	1989 : *F. 3 (GB, 7th)*
• Accident/off :	17	1990 : *F. 3 / Champion*
• Not qualified :	2	*West Surrey*
• Laps in the lead :	1376	1991 : *Lotus / Judd. 2*
• Km in the lead :	6653	*points. 15th of*
• Points scored :	383	*championship.*

F1 CAREER

1993 : *McLaren / Ford. 4 points. 15th of championship.*
1994 : *McLaren / Peugeot. 26 points. 4th of championship.*
1995 : *McLaren / Mercedes. 17 points. 7th of championship.*
1996 : *McLaren / Mercedes. 31 points. 5th of championship.*
1997 : *McLaren / Mercedes. 27 points. 6th of championship.*
1998 : *McLaren / Mercedes. 100 pts.* **World Champion.**
1999 : *McLaren / Mercedes. 76 pts.* **World Champion.**
2000 : *McLaren / Mercedes. 89 points. 2nd of championsh.*

2. David COULTHARD

DRIVER PROFILE

- Name : *COULTHARD*
- First names : *David*
- Nationality : *British*
- Date of birth : *March 27, 1971*
- Place of birth : *Twynholm (Ecosse)*
- Lives in : *Monte Carlo (Monaco)*
- Marital status : *engaged to Heidi*
- Kids : *-*
- Hobbies : *running, cinema, golf*
- Favourite music : *Queen, Phil Collins, Texas*
- Favourite meal : *pasta*
- Favourite drinks : *tea, water*
- Height : *182 cm*
- Weight : *75,5 kg*

STATISTICS | PRIOR TO F1

• Nber of Grand Prix :	107	1983-88 : *Karting*
• Victories :	9	1989 : *Champion junior*
• Pole-positions :	10	*de F. Ford 1600*
• Best laps :	14	1990 : *F. Opel Lotus*
• Accident/off :	13	1991 : *F. 3 GB (2')*
• Not qualified :	0	1992 : *F. 3000 (9')*
• Laps in the lead :	682	1993 : *F. 3000 (3')*
• Km in the lead :	3313	
• Points scored :	294	

F1 CAREER

1994 : *Williams / Renault. 14 points. 8th of championship.*
1995 : *Williams / Renault. 49 points. 3rd of championsh.*
1996 : *McLaren / Mercedes. 18 points. 7th of championship.*
1997 : *McLaren / Mercedes. 36 pts. 3rd of championship.*
1998 : *McLaren / Mercedes. 56 pts. 3rd of championship.*
1999 : *McLaren / Mercedes. 45 points. 4th of championship.*
2000 : *McLaren / Mercedes. 73 points. 3rd of championship.*

Many years from now, long after he has retired, we will remember Mika Hakkinen as a real gentleman. He never has a bad word to say about anyone. Once he steps out of the cockpit of his McLaren, any low blows dealt out by his competitors are immediately forgotten. For the past three seasons, 100 points has constituted the essential minimum requirement for winning the title. This time, because of some failures on the part of his team and a mid-season drop in form, he would stay under that barrier, scoring a mere 89. A shame, as three consecutive titles would have been something to talk about. Although somewhat forgotten with all the euphoria surrounding victory for the red team, he remains dignified and promises to fight hard again in 2001. So we can all look forward to next year. And who knows, maybe fatherhood will make him more chatty.

He enjoyed a very good start to the season right up to the French Grand Prix, finishing all the races between first and third place. And then.... well very little actually. The reason is hard to find. He had the same top speed, the same car as Hakkinen, who only out-qualified him by the smallest of margins. Then, some strategies which he himself described as "risky" went some way to explain his downfall. But more importantly, the downturn in his fortunes corresponded with the upturn in those of his Finnish team-mate. From then on, what has to assume he suffered from a sort of Hakkinen complex. But that does not explain the way Schumacher and Hakkinen simply destroyed the opposition in the last two races, something for which Coulthard only rarely showed any aptitude.

In 1999, Olivier Panis took something of a risk, putting his racing career on hold, joining McLaren as the team's test and reserve driver. But it paid off, as he bounced back to drive for BAR in 2001. Ron Dennis and both his drivers had nothing but praise for what the Frenchman had accomplished.

**McLAREN-MERCEDES MP4/15
DAVID COULTHARD
MONACO GRAND PRIX**

McLaren-Mercedes MP4/15

SPECIFICATION

- Chassis : *McLaren MP4-15*
- Engine : *Mercedes-Benz V10 FO-110 J*
- Wheels : *Enkei*
- Tyres : *Bridgestone*
- Fuel / oil : *Mobil*
- Brakes (discs) : *Carbone Industrie*
- Brakes (calipers) : *AP Racing*
- Transmission : *McLaren 6 gears, semi-autom.*
- Radiators : *McLaren / Calsonic / Marston*
- Plugs / battery : *NGK / GS*
- Shock absorbers : *McLaren*
- Suspensions : *push rods/torsion bar*
- Dry weight : *600 kg, including driver/camera*
- Longueur : *not revealed*
- Front track : *not revealed*
- Rear track : *not revealed*

TEAM PROFILE

- Address : *McLaren International Ltd.*
  Woking Business Park
  Albert Drive, Sheerwater
  Woking, Surrey GU21 5JY
  England
- Telephone : *(44) 1483 711 311*
- Fax : *(44) 1483 711 448*
- Web : *www.mclaren.net*
- Established in : *1963*
- First Grand Prix : *Monaco 1966*
- General director : *Ron Dennis*
- Technical director : *Adrian Newey*
- Team-manager : *Jo Ramirez*
- Nber of employees : *280*
- Sponsors : *Reemtsma(West), Hugo Boss,*
  Tag Heuer, Finlandia, Schweppes

STATISTICS

- Number of Grand Prix : 509
- Number of victories : 130
- Number of pole-positions : 110
- Number of best laps during the race : 99
- Number of drivers' world titles : 11
- Number of constructors' titles : 8
- Total number of points scored : 2481,5

POSITION IN WORLD CHAMPIONSHIP

1966 : 7th – 3 points	1978 : 7th – 15 points	1990 : 1st – 121 points
1967 : 8th – 1 points	1979 : 7th – 15 points	1991 : 1st – 139 points
1968 : 2nd – 51 points	1980 : 7th – 11 points	1992 : 2nd – 99 points
1969 : 4th – 40 points	1981 : 6th – 28 points	1993 : 2nd – 84 points
1970 : 4th – 35 points	1982 : 2nd – 69 points	1994 : 4th – 42 points
1971 : 6th – 10 points	1983 : 5th – 34 points	1995 : 4th – 30 points
1972 : 3rd – 47 points	1984 : 1st – 143.5 points	1996 : 4th – 49 points
1973 : 3rd – 58 points	1985 : 1st – 90 points	1997 : 4th – 63 points
1974 : 1st – 73 points	1986 : 2nd – 96 points	1998 : 1st – 156 points
1975 : 3rd – 53 points	1987 : 2nd – 76 points	1999 : 2nd – 124 points
1976 : 2nd – 74 points	1988 : 1st – 199 points	2000 : 2nd – 152 points
1977 : 3rd – 60 points	1989 : 1st – 141 points	

The best car after all

McLaren without a title to its name is something that had not happened since 1997. Does it signal the start of lean times? It's hard to say, but it is very unlikely given the high quality of the engine, chassis and aerodynamic development which has characterised the past few seasons. Added to that, the team has some of the best brains and a technical team which is a major asset. If the Williams-BMW F23 progresses in the same way that the team has evolved this year, then it could come and challenge the established Ferrari-McLaren order, which we have seen too much of recently. But with over 100 points less than the two leaders after the race in Sepang, the task is enormous. 2001 should see McLaren move from its old Woking base to the new Paragon super-site. Could that disrupt their progress? With titles won or lost on a matter of seconds, it would only need a slight distraction to make them losers once again. And one should not forget that Ferrari will continue to make progress.

TEST DRIVERS 2000

- Olivier PANIS (F)

SUCCESSION OF DRIVERS 2000

- Mika HÄKKINEN : *alls Grand Prix*
- David COULTHARD : *alls Grand Prix*

Ferrari

3. Michael SCHUMACHER

DRIVER PROFILE

- Name : *SCHUMACHER*
- First names : *Michael*
- Nationality : *German*
- Date of birth : *January 3, 1969*
- Place of birth : *Hürth-Hermühlheim (D)*
- Lives in : *Vufflens-le-Château (CH)*
- Marital status : *married to Corinna*
- Kids : *two kids (Gina, Mick)*
- Hobbies : *karting, watches, cinema*
- Favourite music : *Tina Turner, rock*
- Favourite meal : *italian food*
- Favourite drinks : *apple juice with mineral water*
- Height : *174 cm*
- Weight : *75 kg*

STATISTICS

		PRIOR TO F1
Nber of Grand Prix :	145	1984 : *German junior*
Victories :	44	*karting Champion*
Pole-positions :	32	1987 : *European karting*
Best laps :	41	*Champion*
Accident/off :	20	1988 : *German Champion*
Not qualified :	0	*of F. Ford*
Laps in the lead :	2561	1990-91 : *Sportscar*
Km in the lead :	11783	*championship with*
Points scored :	678	*Mercedes*

F1 CAREER

1992 : *Benetton / Ford. 53 points. 3rd of championship.*
1993 : *Benetton / Ford. 52 points. 4th of championship.*
1994 : *Benetton / Ford. 92 points.* **World Champion**
1995 : *Benetton/Renault. 102 pts.* **World Champion**
1996 : *Ferrari. 49 points. 3rd of championship.*
1997 : *Ferrari. 78 points. Excluded of championship.*
1998 : *Ferrari. 86 points. 2nd of championship.*
1999 : *Ferrari. 44 points. 5th of championship.*
2000 : *Ferrari. 108 points.* **World Champion**

4. Rubens BARRICHELLO

DRIVER PROFILE

- Name : *BARRICHELLO*
- First names : *Rubens Gonçalves*
- Nationality : *Brazilian*
- Date of birth : *May 23, 1972*
- Place of birth : *São Paulo (BRE)*
- Lives in : *Monte Carlo (Monaco)*
- Marital status : *married to Silvana*
- Kids : -
- Hobbies : *jet-ski*
- Favourite music : *pop, rock*
- Favourite meal : *pasta*
- Favourite drinks : *Pepsi light*
- Height : *172 cm*
- Weight : *77 kg*

STATISTICS

		PRIOR TO F1
Nber of Grand Prix :	130	1981-88 : *Karting (5 times*
Victories :	1	*Brazilian*
Pole-positions :	3	*Champion)*
Best laps :	3	1989 : *F. Ford 1600 (3rd)*
Accident/off :	21	1990 : *Champion Opel*
Not qualified :	0	*Lotus Euroseries*
Laps in the lead :	133	1991 : *Champion F. 3 (GB)*
Km in the lead :	641	1992 : *F. 3000*
Points scored :	139	

F1 CAREER

1993 : *Jordan / Hart. 2 points. 17th of championship.*
1994 : *Jordan / Hart. 19 points. 6th of championship.*
1995 : *Jordan / Peugeot. 11 points. 11th of championship.*
1996 : *Jordan / Peugeot. 14 points. 8th of championship.*
1997 : *Stewart / Ford. 6 points. 13th of championship.*
1998 : *Stewart / Ford. 4 points. 12th of championship.*
1999 : *Stewart / Ford. 21 points. 7th of championship.*
2000 : *Ferrari. 62 points. 4th of championship.*

△ *It took Jean Todt seven years to deliver his promise to Ferrari boss Luca di Montezemolo to put the Scuderia back on the rails. Having taken the Constructors's title in 1999, total success finally came their way in 2000, with both titles in the bag.*

Michael Schumacher has finally acquired his third world champion's crown. After those of 1994 and 1995, the man who carries the mantle of «the best driver in the world» has now picked up the diploma which accompanies it. He seems more mature and solid than before. In the past, he had won in circumstances that left something to be desired, but not this time. Hakkinen ended a run of twelve races in the points with a retirement in Indianapolis. Schumacher won and his lead grew to eight points. In Suzuka, he rammed home the advantage thanks to a bit of rain and a perfect strategy. He deserved it and his was undoubtedly the best performance of 2000. Even Mika Hakkinen admitted as much.

It might seem harsh to describe a season in which a driver scores his first grand prix season as average, but that is the impression one gets as Rubens Barrichello rounds off his first season with the Scuderia. Left for dead in Suzuka, he finished fourth, 1m 19s down on is team leader. It might have been hard to swallow and there will be little consolation in thinking he had a better first season with the team than Eddie Irvine, given the way the team has evolved since those days. He was closer in qualifying and, in Silverstone at least, he could have added one more win to his record sheet. The real question is how he would shape up against Hakkinen. On three occasions he has wound up second to Schumacher, which suggests he can beat the Finn and he did out-qualify the great Schumacher on two occasions.

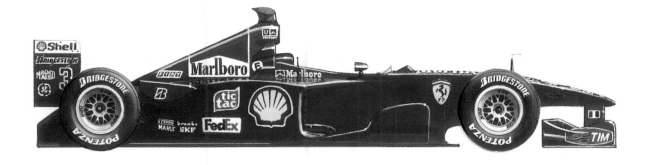

FERRARI F1-2000
MICHAEL SCHUMACHER
BRAZILIAN GRAND PRIX

Ferrari F1-2000

SPECIFICATION

- Chassis : *Ferrari F1-2000*
- Engine : *Ferrari 049- V10*
- Tyres : *Bridgestone*
- Fuel / oil : *Shell*
- Brakes (discs) : *Brembo*
- Brakes (calipers) : *Brembo*
- Transmission : *Ferrari 7 gears, semi-autom.*
- Radiators : *not revealed*
- Plugs : *not revealed*
- Shock absorbers : *not revealed*
- Wheels : *BBS*
- Suspensions : *push rods (ft/bk)*
- Dry weight : *600 kg, including driver/camera*
- Wheelbase : *3010 mm*
- Total length : *4397 mm*
- Total height : *959 mm*
- Front track : *1490 mm*
- Rear track : *1405 mm*

TEAM PROFILE

- Address : *Ferrari SpA*
  Via A. Ascari 55-57
  41053 Maranello (MO)
  Italia
- Telephone : *(39) 0536 94 91 11*
- Fax : *(39) 0536 94 64 88*
- Web : *www.ferrari.it*
- Established in : *1929*
- First Grand Prix : *Monaco 1950*
- General director : *Luca Di Montezemolo*
- Technical director : *Ross Brawn*
  Paolo Martinelli (moteurs)
- Chief designer : *Rory Byrne*
- Team-manager : *Jean Todt*
- Chief mechanic : *Nigel Stepney*
- Nber of employees : *430*
- Sponsors : *Marlboro, Fiat, Shell, Fedex*

TEST DRIVERS 2000

- Luca BADOER (I)

SUCCESSION OF DRIVERS 2000

- M. SCHUMACHER : *alls Grand Prix*
- Rubens BARRICHELLO : *alls Grand Prix*

STATISTICS

- Number of Grand Prix : 636
- Number of victories : 135
- Number of pole-positions : 137
- Number of best laps during the race : 144
- Number of drivers' world titles : 10
- Number of constructors' titles : 10
- Total number of points scored : 2513.5

POSITION IN WORLD CHAMPIONSHIP

1958 : 2nd – 40 points	1973 : 6th – 12 points	1988 : 2nd – 65 points
1959 : 2nd – 32 points	1974 : 2nd – 65 points	1989 : 3rd – 59 points
1960 : 3rd – 24 points	1975 : 1st – 72,5 points	1990 : 2nd – 110 points
1961 : 1st – 40 points	1976 : 1st – 83 points	1991 : 3rd – 55,5 points
1962 : 5th – 18 points	1977 : 1st – 95 points	1992 : 4th – 21 points
1963 : 4th – 26 points	1978 : 2nd – 58 points	1993 : 4th – 23 points
1964 : 1st – 45 points	1979 : 1st – 113 points	1994 : 3rd – 71 points
1965 : 4th – 26 points	1980 : 10th – 8 points	1995 : 3rd – 73 points
1966 : 2nd – 31 points	1981 : 5th – 34 points	1996 : 2nd – 70 points
1967 : 4th – 20 points	1982 : 1st – 74 points	1997 : 2nd – 102 points
1968 : 4th – 32 points	1983 : 1st – 89 points	1998 : 2nd – 133 points
1969 : 5th – 7 points	1984 : 2nd – 57,5 points	1999 : 1st - 128 points
1970 : 2nd – 55 points	1985 : 2nd – 82 points	2000 : 1st – 170 points
1971 : 4th – 33 points	1986 : 4th – 37 points	
1972 : 4th – 33 points	1987 : 4th – 53 points	

Second title in a row and the tenth in its history – a new record

There is little to add to everything that has been said and written about Ferrari's second consecutive Constructors' title. In 1996, they did not have the best car but with Schumacher allegedly worth half a second a lap, they started to put their house in order. Since 1997, they have been in the running right down to the wire and that signified the start of a new era for the team. This year was near perfect with a record ten wins, delivered partly because Hakkinen took ages to get points on the board and then seemed to lose form mid-season. But above all, the F1-2000 was simply too quick and too reliable and the big difference this year was that it seemed equally well suited to just about every type of circuit; fast or slow, high or low downforce, it seemed to make little difference. Towards the end of the summer, a tendency to be harder on its tyres than the McLaren was its only weak point, but strategically the Italians always seemed to have the upper hand. An accomplished performance.

Jordan Mugen Honda

This was not a good year for the German. In 1999, he was one of the stars of the show, winning races, never making any mistakes and challenging for the title until a few races from the end. This year, the talented driver found it harder to cope with the technical problems and the difficulties of setting up a tricky chassis. He was often out-performed by his younger and less experienced team mate. In qualifying Trulli often had the edge, although the German could be more consistent in the races themselves. But when the chips were down, the wheel seemed to stop on Trulli's number more often. Frentzen is nothing if not resilient and can turn the situation around next year.

5. Heinz-Harald FRENTZEN

DRIVER PROFILE

- Name : FRENTZEN
- First names : Heinz-Harald
- Nationality : German
- Date of birth : May 18, 1967
- Place of birth : Mönchengladbach (D)
- Lives in : Monte Carlo (Monaco)
- Marital status : married to Tanja
- Kids : one girl (Léa)
- Hobbies : meet and have diner with his friends
- Favourite music : U2, soul, rap
- Favourite meal : fish, paëlla, pasta
- Favourite drinks : mineral water
- Height : 174 cm
- Weight : 64,5 kg

STATISTICS | PRIOR TO F1

• Nber of Grand Prix :	113	1980-85 : Karting
• Victories :	3	1886-87 : F. Ford 2000
• Pole-positions :	2	1988 : Champion F. Opel
• Best laps :	6	Lotus
• Accident/off :	21	1989 : F3 Germany
• Not qualified :	0	1990-91 : F3000
• Laps in the lead :	149	1992-93 : F3000 of Japan
• Km in the lead :	745	
• Points scored :	153	

F1 CAREER

1994 : Sauber / Mercedes. 7 points. 13th of championship.
1995 : Sauber / Ford. 15 points. 9th of championship.
1996 : Sauber / Ford. 7 points. 12th of championship.
1997 : Williams / Renault. 42 pts. 2nd of championship.
1998 : Williams / Mécachrome. 17 pts. 7th of championship.
1999 : Jordan / Mugen-Honda. 54 pts. 3rd of championship.
2000 : Jordan / Mugen-Honda. 11 pts. 9th of championship.

6. Jarno TRULLI

DRIVER PROFILE

- Name : TRULLI
- First names : Jarno
- Nationality : Italian
- Date of birth : July 13, 1974
- Place of birth : Pescara (I)
- Lives in : Francavilla (I)
- Marital status : single
- Kids : -
- Hobbies : tennis, kart, swimming
- Favourite music : Vasco Rossi, Elton John
- Favourite meal : pizza
- Favourite drinks : Coca-Cola
- Height : 173 cm
- Weight : 60 kg

STATISTICS | PRIOR TO F1

• Nber of Grand Prix :	76	1988-93: Kart 100
• Victories :	0	6 time champion (ITA)
• Pole-positions :	0	1991 : World Champion
• Best laps :	0	FSA (100)
• Accident/off :	13	1994 : World Champion
• Not qualified :	0	FC (125)
• Laps in the lead :	37	1995 : Champ. F3 (GER), 4e
• Km in the lead :	160	1996 : Champ. F3 (GER), 1er
• Points scored :	17	1997 : Minardi half-saison
		(0pt)

F1 CAREER

1997 : Prost / Mugen Honda. 3 points. 15th of champ.
1998 : Prost / Peugeot. 1 point. 15th of championship.
1999 : Prost / Peugeot. 7 point. 11th of championship.
2000 : Jordan / Mugen-Honda. 6 pts. 10th of championship.

It is hard to believe that the youngster has already been in Formula One for four years. When he first pitched up in the paddocks, people commented on his resemblance to the late Ayrton Senna. Perhaps the similarity is more than physical. Right from the start of a grand prix weekend, he is a picture of studied concentration, although he lacks the Brazilian's stand-offish demeanour. He thinks things through and shuts himself off from the outside world before giving it his total commitment. It is very impressive as his level of fitness which rivals that of Michael Schumacher. He never bothers with a drinks bottle during a race and finishes even the toughest grand prix looking fresh as a dairy. He has the makings of a champion and he is ready to win grands prix, judging by his qualifying performances, if he is given the equipment to do it next season.

Compared with 1999, the team made heavy weather of 2000. Recruiting Jarno Trulli was not enough to maintain the team's third place in the Constructors' table. The highpoint of Eddie's year was securing the same works Honda engine as BAR for the future.

▽

JORDAN-MUGEN HONDA EJ10
HEINZ-HARALD FRENTZEN
BRAZILIAN GRAND PRIX

Jordan-Mugen Honda EJ10

SPECIFICATION

- Chassis : Jordan EJ 10
- Engine : Mugen-Honda V10 MF 301 HE
- Tyres : Bridgestone
- Wheels : OZ Racing
- Fuel / oil : not revealed
- Brakes (discs) : Carbone Industrie/Brembo
- Brakes (calipers) : Brembo
- Transmission : Jordan 6 gears
- Radiators : Secan / Jordan
- Plugs / battery : NGK / Fiamm
- Shock absorbers : Penske
- Suspensions : push rods carbon (ft/bk)
- Dry weight : 600 kg, including driver/camera
- Wheelbase : 3050 mm
- Front track : 1500 mm
- Rear track : 1418 mm

TEAM PROFILE

- Address : Jordan Grand Prix
  Buckingham Road, Silverstone,
  Northants NN12 8TJ
  England
- Telephone : (44) 1327 850 800
- Fax : (44) 1327 857 993
- Web : www.jordangp.com
- Established in : 1981
- First Grand Prix : USA 1991
- General director : Eddie Jordan
- Technical director : Mike Gascoyne
- Team-manager : Trevor Foster
- Chief mechanic : Tim Edwards
- Nber of employees : 202
- Sponsors : Benson&Hedges, Master Card, HP

STATISTICS

- Number of Grand Prix : 163
- Number of victories : 3
- Number of pole-positions : 2
- Number of best laps during the race : 2
- Number of drivers' world titles : 0
- Number of constructors' titles : 0
- Total number of points scored : 230

POSITION IN WORLD CHAMPIONSHIP

1991 : 5th – 13 points
1992 : 11th – 1 point
1993 : 10th – 3 points
1994 : 5th – 28 points
1995 : 6th – 21 points
1996 : 5th – 22 points
1997 : 5th – 33 points
1998 : 4th – 34 points
1999 : 3rd – 61 points
2000 : 6th – 17 points

A bad year but a bright future

In 1999, Jordan finished third in the championship and at the start of this season there was brave talk of challenging the top two teams. With hindsight, that was a rash promise, but any chance of giving it credibility went out the window courtesy of a gear-box that had not only mechanical problems, but electrical ones too. The team had hoped to progress by grasping radical technologies in these areas. It was a brave gamble which did not pay off, as it took half the season to solve. The team was also desperately unlucky on several occasions with stupid problems and their drivers involved in accidents which were not of their own making. The high point was Jarno Trulli starting from the front row on two occasions in Monaco and Spa. More importantly, the French GP found Eddie Jordan puffing his chest out with pride as he announced a new engine deal with the great Honda factory. The future looks much better than the past. In the short term, the team needs to regroup around a new technical director, after Mike Gascoyne's departure for pastures new at Benetton. It is also planning to expand its rather basic Silverstone factory to raise its game to match Honda's expectations. While it celebrated its tenth anniversary of F1 participation, the eleventh year should give greater cause for rejoicing.

TEST DRIVERS 2000

- Tomas ENGE (TSC)

SUCCESSION OF DRIVERS 2000

- H.-H. FRENTZEN : alls Grand Prix
- Jarno TRULLI : alls Grand Prix

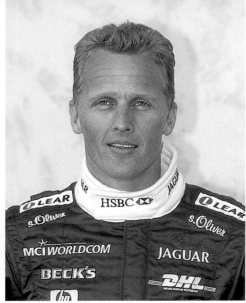

7. Eddie IRVINE

DRIVER PROFILE

- Name : *IRVINE*
- First names : *Edmund*
- Nationality : *British*
- Date of birth : *November 10, 1965*
- Place of birth : *Newtownards (IRE)*
- Lives in : *Dublin (IR)*
- Marital status : *single*
- Kids : *one girl (Zoé)*
- Hobbies : *fishing, golf, snowboard*
- Favourite music : *rock, Van Morrison*
- Favourite meal : *chinese*
- Favourite drinks : *beer Miller*
- Height : *178 cm*
- Weight : *70 kg*

STATISTICS | PRIOR TO F1

- Nber of Grand Prix : *113*
- Victories : *4*
- Pole-positions : *0*
- Best laps : *1*
- Accident/off : *29*
- Not qualified : *0*
- Laps in the lead : *156*
- Km in the lead : *838*
- Points scored : *177*

PRIOR TO F1
1983-87 : F. Ford 1600
1988 : F.3 GB
1989 : F.3000
1990 : F.3000 (3ᵉ)
1991 : F.3000 Japan (7ᵉ)
1992 : F.3000 Japan (8ᵉ)
1993 : F.3000 Japan (2ᵉ)

F1 CAREER

1993 : *Jordan / Hart. 0 point.*
1994 : *Jordan / Hart. 6 points. 14th of championship.*
1995 : *Jordan / Peugeot. 10 points. 12th of championship.*
1996 : *Ferrari. 11 points. 10th of championship.*
1997 : *Ferrari. 24 points. 7th of championship.*
1998 : *Ferrari. 47 points. 4th of championship.*
1999 : *Ferrari. 74 points. 2nd of championship*
2000 : *Ferrari. 4 points. 13th of championship*

8. Johnny HERBERT

DRIVER PROFILE

- Name : *HERBERT*
- First names : *Johnny*
- Nationality : *British*
- Date of birth : *June 27, 1964*
- Place of birth : *Romford (GB)*
- Lives in : *Monte Carlo (Monaco)*
- Marital status : *married to Rebecca*
- Kids : *two girls (Amelia, Chloe)*
- Hobbies : *golf, squash, fishing*
- Favourite music : *rock, pop, Eric Clapton*
- Favourite meal : *pasta*
- Favourite drinks : *apple juice*
- Height : *167 cm*
- Weight : *69 kg*

STATISTICS | PRIOR TO F1

- Nber of Grand Prix : *161*
- Victories : *3*
- Pole-positions : *0*
- Best laps : *0*
- Accident/off : *25*
- Not qualified : *3*
- Laps in the lead : *44*
- Km in the lead : *226*
- Points scored : *98*

PRIOR TO F1
1984-85 : F. Ford 1600
1986 : F. Ford 2000
1987 : GB Champion de F. 3
1988 : F3000
1989 : Benetton / Ford & Tyrrell / Ford. 0 point.
1990 : Lotus / Lamborghini. 0 point (2 GP).

F1 CAREER

1991 : *Lotus / Judd. 0 point.*
1992 : *Lotus / Ford. 2 points. 14e du championnat.*
1993 : *Lotus / Ford. 11 points. 8e du championnat.*
1994 : *Lotus / Honda. 0 point.*
1995 : *Benetton / Renault. 45 points. 4e du championnat.*
1996 : *Sauber / Ford. 4 points. 14e du championnat.*
1997 : *Sauber / Petronas. 15 points. 10e du championnat.*
1998 : *Sauber / Petronas. 1 point. 15e du championnat.*
1999 : *Stewart / Ford. 15 points. 8e du championnat.*
2000 : *Jaguar. 0 point.*

The Irishman went from being the runner-up in the 1999 championship to thirteenth this year with just four points to his name. A huge salary was part of the attraction but shrugging off the mantle of Michael Schumacher's whipping boy was probably a greater incentive. Sadly, the R1 had all sorts of problems which were never solved satisfactorily. Occasionally, when it all came together, there were flashes of the old Eddie. Encouragingly, the light at the end of the tunnel got brighter towards the end of the season and he showed well in both Suzuka and Sepang. That might give him cause for optimism for the future.

«Everyone is welcome to my farewell party and presents will be appreciated- walking sticks, motorised wheel chairs....» Even in Sepang for the final race of the season, Johnny Herbert had not lost his sense of humour. Having won three grands prix and the Le Mans 24 Hours, the Englishman was already setting his sights on a career in Indy racing in the USA, with a view to winning the Indianapolis 500, the last dream on his list. Always ambitious and very determined, everyone in the sport will miss his good humour and ready smile. If there was a prize for the unluckiest driver in the sport, he would definitely be in the running for the gold medal.

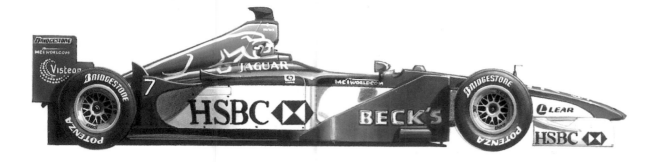

**JAGUAR-COSWORTH R1
EDDIE IRVINE
MONACO GRAND PRIX**

Jaguar R1

SPECIFICATION

- Chassis : *Jaguar R1*
- Engine : *Cosworth V10 CR-2*
- Tyres : *Bridgestone*
- Wheels : *BBS*
- Fuel / oil : *Texaco / Havoline*
- Brakes (discs) : *Carbone Industrie*
- Brakes (calipers) : *AP Racing*
- Transmission : *Jaguar 6 gears, semi-autom.*
- Radiators : *IMI*
- Plugs : *Champion / JRL*
- Shock absorbers : *Jaguart / Penske*
- Suspensions : *Upper, carbon fibre*
- Dry weight : *not revealed*
- Wheelbase : *not revealed*
- Front track : *1469 mm*
- Rear track : *1408 mm*
- Total length : *4500 mm*

TEAM PROFILE

- Address : *Jaguar Racing Ltd
  Bradbourne Drive, Tilbrook,
  Milton Keynes, MK7 8BJ
  England*
- Telephone : *(44) 1908 27 97 00*
- Fax : *(44) 1908 27 97 11*
- Web : *www.jaguar-racing.com*
- Established in : *2000*
- First Grand Prix : *Australia 2000*
- General director : *Neil Ressler*
- Technical director : *Gary Anderson*
- Team-manager : *David Stubbs*
- Chief mechanic : *Dave boys*
- Nber of employees : *250*
- Sponsor : *HSBC, DHL, HP, Texaco*

STATISTICS

- Number of Grand Prix :   17
- Number of victories :   0
- Number of pole-positions :   0
- Number of best laps during the race :   0
- Number of drivers' world titles :   0
- Number of constructors' titles :   0
- Total number of points scored :   4

POSITION IN WORLD CHAMPIONSHIP

2000 : *9th – 4 points*

△

The end of an era. Johnny Herbert quit F1 for pastures new, maybe in CART and Jackie Stewart slipped into the background, even if he continued to attend most of the races.

Death by marketing

By the end of 1999, the young Stewart GP team was coming together nicely. It had a good little car and a loyal, small and effective team. Then Ford came along, Jackie Stewart took a back seat, his son Paul was sidelined through illness and the team fell apart. It was killed by a top-heavy Jaguar marketing operation that had the tail wagging the dog. Racing had become of secondary importance to having its drivers take part in a million and one meaningless promotions. The appointment of Neil Ressler, a top man at Ford but at the end of his working life, did nothing to turn the situation around. It did not help that the R1 was no match for its predecessor, suffered reliability problems and was a treacherous piece of kit to drive. While all was glossy on the surface, especially the team's monstrous motorhome, it did not even have a wind tunnel, using one in the USA instead; hardly the handiest of journeys from Milton Keynes. Former Indy 500 winner, and team boss Bobby Rahal might make a difference for 2001, but nothing is guaranteed in this sport.

TEST DRIVERS 2000
- Luciano BURTI (BRE)

SUCCESSION OF DRIVERS 2000
- Eddie IRVINE :   *alls Grand Prix except AUT*
- Luciano BURTI :   *AUT*
- Johnny HERBERT :   *alls Grand Prix*

Williams-BMW

9. Ralf SCHUMACHER

DRIVER PROFILE

- Name : *SCHUMACHER*
- First names : *Ralf*
- Nationality : *German*
- Date of birth : *June 30, 1975*
- Place of birth : *Hürth-Hermühlheim (D)*
- Lives in : *Monte Carlo (Monaco)*
- Marital status : *single*
- Kids : *-*
- Hobbies : *karting, bachgammon*
- Favourite music : *soft rock*
- Favorite meal : *pasta*
- Favourite drinks : *apple juice with mineral water*
- Height : *178 cm*
- Weight : *73 kg*

STATISTICS

		PRIOR TO F1
• Nber of Grand Prix :	66	1978-92 : *Karting*
• Victories :	0	1993 : *Jr. Champ. ADAC*
• Pole-positions :	0	1994 : *Champ. F. 3 (D, 3rd)*
• Best laps :	1	1995 : *Champ. F. 3 (D,*
• Accident/off :	17	*2nd), winner world*
• Not qualified :	0	*final F.3 in Macao*
• Laps in the lead :	8	1996 : *F. 3000 Champion*
• Km in the lead :	36	*(Japan)*
• Points scored :	86	

F1 CAREER

1997 : *Jordan / Peugeot. 13 points. 11th of championship.*
1998 : *Jordan / Mugen-Honda. 14 pts. 10th of champ.*
1999 : *Williams / Supertec. 35 points. 6th of championship.*
2000 : *Williams / BMW. 24 points. 5th of championship.*

10. Jenson BUTTON

DRIVER PROFILE

- Name : *BUTTON*
- First names : *Jenson*
- Nationality : *British*
- Date of birth : *January 19, 1980*
- Place of birth : *Frome (GB)*
- Lives in : *Bicester (GB)*
- Marital status : *single*
- Kids : *-*
- Hobbies : *surfing the Net*
- Favourite music : *techno & disco*
- Favorite meal : *pasta*
- Favourite drinks : *orange juice*
- Height : *182 cm*
- Weight : *72 kg*

STATISTICS

		PRIOR TO F1
• Nber of Grand Prix :	17	1998 : *Champion Formule*
• Victories :	0	*Ford in England*
• Pole-positions :	0	1999 : *F3*
• Best laps :	0	
• Accident/off :	7	
• Not qualified :	0	
• Laps in the lead :	0	
• Km in the lead :	0	
• Points scored :	12	

F1 CAREER

2000 : *Williams / BMW. 12 points. 8th of championship.*

He might have been out-qualified by his teammate six times out of seventeen, but nothing phases Ralf Schumacher. While everyone banged on about the age or lack of it of his teammate, Michael's little brother is hardly a veteran. And yet he drives like one and his experience paid off and he won the non-Ferrari/McLaren championship, with three podium finishes to his name and 24 points on his scorecard. Ralf has proved that he might well have as much talent as his big brother. Mature and solid, he has proved to be a real racer of the old school. He has also evolved as a person. Gone is the rather surly attitude of his early career. Sometimes he can even be funny. The next stage has to be a race win. There is no doubt he has the ability so now he will be looking to Williams and BMW to provide him with the necessary equipment.

Watching him drive, listening to him speak, seeing him cope with the pressure, it was hard to believe Jenson Button was only twenty and fresh from the British Formula 3 championship. With his former rallycross driving father by his side, the rookie took to F1 like a fish to water. Even his debut in Melbourne didn't phase him, neither did his occasional off-track excursion. He even allowed himself the luxury of picking up a point in his second grand prix. "Buttonmania" took off at Silverstone but it was far from home on tracks like Spa, where he shone in the wet and at Indianapolis where he was on level pegging in terms of circuit knowledge with the rest of the field, that he really proved that he has a great future in the sport. That future means leaving Williams, at least for the next couple of years. He will probably find life with his new masters at Benetton or Renault if you prefer, rather more difficult, but Sir Frank Williams will no doubt be happy to have him back in a couple of years time.

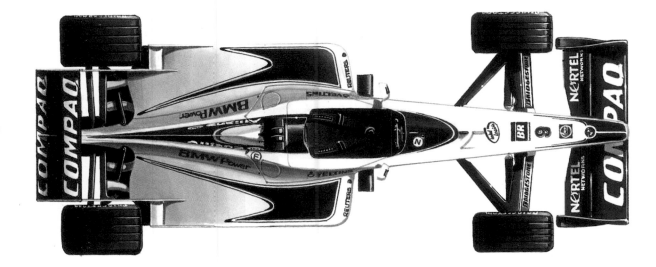

**WILLIAMS BMW FW22
RALF SCHUMACHER
EUROPEAN GRAND PRIX**

Williams BMW FW22

SPECIFICATION

- Chassis : *Williams FW22*
- Engine : *BMW V10 E 41/4*
- Tyres : *Bridgestone*
- Wheels : *OZ Racing*
- Fuel : *Petrobras*
- Brakes (discs) : *Carbone Industrie*
- Brakes (calipers) : *AP Racing*
- Transmission : *Williams 6 gears, semi-autom.*
- Radiators : *not revealed*
- Plugs : *NGK*
- Shock absorbers : *Williams-Penske*
- Suspensions : *Williams-Penske*
- Dry weight : *600 kg, including driver/camera*
- Wheelbase : *3140 mm*
- Front track : *1460 mm*
- Rear track : *1400 mm*
- Total length : *4540 mm*

TEAM PROFILE

- Address : *BMW Williams F1 Grove, Wantage Oxfordshire OX12 0DQ, England*
- Telephone : *(44) 1235 77 77 00*
- Fax : *(44) 1235 77 77 39*
- Web : *www.williamsf1.co.uk*
- Established in : *1969*
- First Grand Prix : *Argentina 1978*
- General director : *Frank Williams*
- Technical director : *Patrick Head*
- Team manager : *Dickie Stanford*
- Chief mechanic : *Carl Gaden*
- Nber of employees : *360*
- Sponsor : *BMW, Compaq, Du Pont*

STATISTICS

- Number of Grand Prix : 428
- Number of victories : 103
- Number of pole-positions : 108
- Number of best laps during the race : 110
- Number of drivers' world titles : 7
- Number of constructors' titles : 9
- Total number of points scored : 2031.5

POSITION IN WORLD CHAMPIONSHIP

1975 : 9th – 6 points	1988 : 7th – 20 points
1976 : not classified	1989 : 2nd – 77 points
1977 : not classified	1990 : 4th – 57 points
1978 : 9th – 11 points	1991 : 2nd – 125 points
1979 : 2nd – 75 points	1992 : 1st – **164 points**
1980 : 1st – **120 points**	1993 : 1st – **168 points**
1981 : 1st – **95 points**	1994 : 1st – **118 points**
1982 : 4th – 58 points	1995 : 2nd – 112 points
1983 : 4th – 38 points	1996 : 1st – **175 points**
1984 : 6th – 25.5 points	1997 : 1st – **123 points**
1985 : 3rd – 71 points	1998 : 3rd – 38 points
1986 : 1st – **141 points**	1999 : 5th – 35 points
1987 : 1st – **137 points**	2000 : 3rd – 36 points

Gerhard Berger handled a change of career with aplomb. He headed up BMW's return to F1, leading them to third place in the Constructors' Championship with Williams. A success for the Bavarian company. ▽

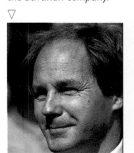

Top of the second division

The new partnership between Williams and BMW was the pleasant surprise of this season, far exceeding what anyone, including the team principals had expected from their first year together. Despite a strong showing, they were still light years away from the top two, Ferrari and McLaren. However, they were clearly better than the rest and their experience when it came to reading race tactics often allowed them to outfox quicker cars come the chequered flag. The FW22 chassis seemed easy to adapt to the demands of different circuits and the BMW V10 which had proved so weak and fragile, found reliability in the nick of time just prior to the first round of the season, allowing Ralf Schumacher to claim third place in Melbourne. No doubt Berger's experience of developing new engines and overcoming insurmountable problems with other teams had a calming effect on his team of novices. 2001 will be a different story and their ambition cannot allow them to live through another year of being a pleasant surprise. They need to start winning.

TEST DRIVERS 2000
- Bruno JUNQUIERA (BRE)

SUCCESSION OF DRIVERS 2000
- Ralf SCHUMACHER : *alls Grand Prix*
- Jenson BUTTON : *alls Grand Prix*

Benetton-Playlife

11. Giancarlo FISICHELLA

DRIVER PROFILE

- Name :   *FISICHELLA*
- First names :   *Giancarlo*
- Nationality :   *Italian*
- Date of birth :   *January 14, 1973*
- Place of birth :   *Rome (I)*
- Lives in :   *Roma et Monte Carlo (Monaco)*
- Marital status :   *engaged to Luna*
- Kids :   *one girl (Carlotta)*
- Hobbies :   *skiing, fishing, football, tennis*
- Favourite music : *Elton John, Renato Zero*
- Favorite meal :   *bucatini alla matriciana (pasta)*
- Favourite drinks : *orange juice*
- Height :   *172 cm*
- Weight :   *64 kg*

STATISTICS

		PRIOR TO F1	
• Nber of Grand Prix :	74	1984-88 :	Karting
• Victories :	0	1989 :	World Champion-
• Pole-positions :	1		ship Karting (4th)
• Best laps :	1	1991 :	F. Alfa Boxer; karting
• Accident/off :	15		(EUR) (2nd)
• Not qualified :	0	1992-94 :	F 3 (ITA),
• Laps in the lead :	35		champion in1994
• Km in the lead :	172	1995 :	DTM/ITC Alfa
• Points scored :	67		Romeo

F1 CAREER

1996 : Minardi / Ford. 0 point.
1997 : Jordan / Peugeot. 20 points. *8th* of championship.
1998 : Benetton / Playlife. 16 points. *9th* of championship.
1999 : Benetton / Playlife. 13 points. *9th* of championship.
2000 : Benetton / Playlife. 18 points. *6th* of championship.

12. Alexander WURZ

DRIVER PROFILE

- Name :   *WURZ*
- First names :   *Alexander*
- Nationality :   *Austrian*
- Date of birth :   *February 15, 1974*
- Place of birth :   *Waidhofen (AUT)*
- Lives in :   *Monte Carlo (Monaco)*
- Marital status :   *engaged to Karin*
- Kids :   *-*
- Hobbies :   *skiing, snowboard, squash*
- Favourite music : *Beatles, Pink Floyd et Rolling Stones*
- Favourite meal :   *pasta*
- Favourite drinks : *apple juice with mineral water*
- Height :   *187 cm*
- Weight :   *74 kg*

STATISTICS

		PRIOR TO F1	
• Nbre de Grands Prix :	52	1989 -90 :	kart (AUS) (2nd)
• Victoires :	0		Middle East KW (4th)
• Pole-positions :	0	1991 :	FFord 1600 (AUS)(1st)
• Meilleurs tours :	1	1992 :	FFord 1600 (D)(1st)
• Accidents/sorties :	7	1993 :	F3 (AUS) champion
• Non-qualifications :	0	1994 :	F3 (D) (2nd)
• Tours en tête :	0	1995 :	F3 (D) (6th)
• Km en tête :	0	1996 :	Le Mans 24H (1st)
• Points marqués :	26		

F1 CAREER

1997 : Benetton / Renault. 4 points. *14th* of championship.
1998 : Benetton / Playlife. 17 points. *7th* of championship.
1999 : Benetton / Playlife. 3 points. *13th* of championship.
2000 : Benetton / Playlife. 2 points. *15th* of championship.

The great white hope, the world champion in the making that was Giancarlo Fisichella a few years back seemed to see his bright light fade a bit this year. Always devilishly quick and occasionally capable of fighting like a lion, the Roman seemed to suffer more than expected from the period of instability that followed Flavio Briatore's return to the helm, until the new team owner reconfirmed his contract for 2001. A good second place in Brazil and two consecutive thirds in Monaco and Canada and then nothing to the end of the season. He made the headlines by clashing with Michael Schumacher at the first corner in Germany and for getting a right royal ticking off from Briatore for turning up late in Indianapolis. He is still quick but he needs to fan the flames of a career that looks like fizzling out.

From Wurz to bad and another jokes about his name, characterise the terrible season the Austrian endured, before finding sanctuary with the job of McLaren test driver for 2001. Maybe his height counted against him as he is fifteen centimetres taller than his team-mate, which represents a weight penalty. But that alone does not go all the way to explaining why Fisichella out-qualified him more than ten times this year, nor why he scored just two points all year long. It was as though, someone flicked a switch in his brain and the Austrian seemed a beaten man before even getting into the cockpit. It must have been hard to live with. He has been thrown a lifeline by McLaren. Will he repeat Olivier Panis' performance by hauling himself out of the water and into another F1 drive in two years time?

He's back. Flavio Briatore was put in charge of paving the way for Renault's return in 2002. In the meantime it was time for some housekeeping. Out went Wurz, who didn't get on with the boss and in comes Button. In 2001, the pressure will be turned up.

▽

BENETTON-PLAYLIFE B200
GIANCARLO FISICHELLA
BRAZILIAN GRAND PRIX

Benetton-Playlife B200

SPECIFICATION

- Chassis : *Benetton B200*
- Engine : *Playlife FB 02*
- Tyres : *Bridgestone*
- Wheels : *BBS*
- Fuel : *Agip*
- Brakes (discs) : *Brembo*
- Brakes (calipers) : *AP Racing*
- Transmission : *Benetton 6 gears, semi-autom.*
- Radiators : *Benetton*
- Plugs : *Champion*
- Shock absorbers : *Dynamics*
- Suspensions : *push rods (ft/bk)*
- Dry weight : *600 kg including driver/camera*
- Wheelbase : *not revealed*
- Front track : *not revealed*
- Rear track : *not revealed*

TEAM PROFILE

- Address : *Benetton F1 Racing Team*
  Whiteways Technical Centre
  Enstone, Chipping Norton
  Oxon OX7 4EE
  England
- Telephone : *(44) 1608 67 80 00*
- Fax : *(44) 1608 67 86 09*
- Web : *www.benettonf1.com*
- Established in : *1970 (under the name Toleman)*
- First Grand Prix : *Italia 1981*
- General director : *Flavio Briatore*
- Technical director : *Pat Symonds*
- Team-manager : *Carlos Nunes*
- Chief mechanic : *Mike Ainsley-Cowlishaw*
- Nber of employees : *320*
- Sponsors : *Mild Seven, Playlife, Korean Air,*
  Agip

STATISTICS

• Number of Grand Prix :	300
• Number of victories :	26
• Number of pole-positions :	16
• Number of best laps during the race :	38
• Number of drivers' world titles :	2
• Number of constructors' titles :	1
• Total number of points scored :	867.5

POSITION IN WORLD CHAMPIONSHIP

1981 : *not classified*	1991 : *4th – 38,5 points*
1982 : *not classified*	1992 : *3rd – 91 points*
1983 : *9th – 10 points*	1993 : *3rd – 72 points*
1984 : *7th – 16 points*	1994 : *2nd – 103 points*
1985 : *not classified*	1995 : ***1st – 137 points***
1986 : *6th – 19 points*	1996 : *3rd – 68 points*
1987 : *5th – 28 points*	1997 : *3rd – 67 points*
1988 : *3rd – 39 points*	1998 : *5th – 33 points*
1989 : *4th – 39 points*	1999 : *6th – 16 points*
1990 : *3rd – 71 points*	2000 : *4th – 20 points*

Time to get serious

Benetton had been going downhill for several seasons now. The days of Berger and Alesi had not exactly brought success, in the wake of the departure of wunderkind Michael Schumacher. The fact the German had taken the big brains of the technical department with him to Maranello did not help either. Gradually the team seemed to sink further and further into anonymity, a strange state of affairs for what used to be the liveliest team in the pit lane. It appeared to have lost not only the will to win, but also the will to live. Then, early in 1999, Renault announced it had bought out the Benetton family's interest and would rename the team as Renault in 2002. In the short term, the French manufacturer also returned the flamboyant Flavio Briatore to his role as team leader. It made little impact on this year's result sheet. Next season, the highly rated Mike Gascoyne will head up the technical department, having been prised away from Jordan with a big bag of gold. In the first instance, Briatore tried to tempt Jacques Villeneuve back to renew his winning ways with Renault, who powered the Canadian to his 1997 title with Williams. Having failed, he settled on Jenson Button and re-confirmed Fisichella. 2001 should be better, but not by much.

TEST DRIVERS 2000
- Hidetoshi MITSUSADA (JAP)

SUCCESSION OF DRIVERS 2000
- Giancarlo FISICHELLA : *alls Grand Prix*
- Alexander WURZ : *alls Grand Prix*

18. Pedro de la ROSA

DRIVER PROFILE

- Name : de la ROSA
- First names : Pedro
- Nationality : Spanish
- Date of birth : February 24, 1971
- Place of birth : Barcelone (ESP)
- Lives in : Barcelone (ESP)
- Marital status : engaged to Maria
- Kids : -
- Hobbies : sports
- Favourite music : Mecano
- Favourite meal : paëlla, pasta
- Favourite drinks : mineral water
- Height : 178 cm
- Weight : 74 kg

STATISTICS

		PRIOR TO F1
• Nber of Grand Prix :	33	since 86 : Formule Fiat -
• Victories :	0	F.3 - F.3000
• Pole-positions :	0	1997 : 3rd of champion-
• Best laps :	0	ship Spark Plug
• Accident/off :	9	World Drivers
• Not qualified :	0	
• Laps in the lead :	0	
• Km in the lead :	0	
• Points scored :	3	

F1 CAREER

1998 : Jordan. Test driver
1999 : Arrows. 1 point. 17th of championship
2000 : Arrows. 2 points. 16th of championship

19. Jos VERSTAPPEN

DRIVER PROFILE

- Name : Verstappen
- First names : Joshannes Franciscus
- Nationality : Dutch
- Date of birth : March 4, 1972
- Place of birth : Montford (NL)
- Lives in : Monte Carlo (MC)
- Marital status : married to Sophie
- Kids : one girl and one boy
- Hobbies : go-kart
- Favourite music : pop, UB40
- Favourite meal : pasta and dutch dish
- Favourite drinks : Coca cola
- Height : 175 cm
- Weight : 73 kg

STATISTICS

		PRIOR TO F1
• Nber of Grand Prix :	81	1980-91 : karting
• Victories :	0	1992 : Champion F. Opel
• Pole-positions :	0	Lotus
• Best laps :	0	1993 : Champion
• Accident/off :	0	Zandvoort Marlboro
• Not qualified :	0	Masters F3
• Laps in the lead :	0	& Champion F3 (GER)
• Km in the lead :	0	
• Points scored :	16	

F1 CAREER

1994 : Benetton / Ford. 10 pts. 10th of championship
1995 : Simtek / Ford. 5 GP, 0 point
1996 : Arrows / Hart. 1 pt. 16th of championship
1997 : Tyrrell / Ford. 0 point
1998 : Stewart / Ford. 9 GP disputés 0 point
2000 : Arrows. 5 point. 12th of championship

While all the hullabaloo and media attention focusses on the front of the grid, there have been some solid performance further down the grid and one of them has come from this likeable Spaniard. Pedro has won in every category he has entered, so as he says himself, "why not in F1?" He ended the season with just two little points but that does not reveal how often he was in the thick of it, how often he did better than he should have done. He is still learning the art of being a grand prix driver and is improving all the time. Generally, he outpaced his team-mate in qualifying, although this did not always translate into results come Sunday afternoon. He comes with a big bag of Spanish gold and, as long as next year's Peugeot engine (rebadged as AMT) does not become a millstone around his neck, then he could be ready to make the leap to a front running team in a couple of years. Either that, or will simply disappear from view.

The likeable Dutchman has dipped in and out of Formula 1 so often, it is hard to believe he is still only twenty eight. Apart from an early stint with Benetton, he has swum around the lower end of the paddock before finally finding a suitable pond with Arrows. After an enforced sabbatical in 1999, he was terribly unfit when he started the last season. But he gradually got stronger and formed an effective partnership with De La Rosa. There were some great drives, most notably to fourth place in the Italian Grand Prix and finally he seems to have got out of the habit of throwing the car into the scenery. He is still prone to the odd unforced error however. Confirmed for another year with Walkinshaw's crew, the biggest question mark over his career will be that dreaded Peugeot power unit.

ARROWS A21
PEDRO DE LA ROSA
EUROPEAN GRAND PRIX

Arrows A21

SPECIFICATION

- Chassis : Arrows A 21
- Engine : Supertec V10 FB02
- Tyres : Bridgestone
- Wheels : BBS
- Fuel / oil : Arrows
- Brakes (discs) : Carbone Industrie
- Brakes (calipers) : AP Racing / Arrows
- Transmission : Xtrac/Arrows 6 gears, semi-auto.
- Radiators : not revealed
- Plugs / battery : Champion/ Fiamm
- Shock absorbers : Dynamics
- Suspensions : push rods (ft/bk)
- Dry weight : 600 kg, including driver/camera
- Wheelbase : 2995 mm
- Front track : 1465 mm
- Rear track : 1410 mm
- Total length : 4430 mm

TEAM PROFILE

- Address : Arrows F1 Team
  Leafield Technical Centre
  Witney, Oxon OX8 5PF
  England
- Telephone : (44) 1993 87 10 00
- Fax : (44) 1993 87 10 87
- Web : www.arrows.co.uk
- Established in : 1977
- First Grand Prix : Brazil 1978
- General director : Tom Walkinshaw
- Technical director : Mike Coughlan
- Team-manager : Steve BNielsen
- Chief mechanic : Stuart Cowie
- Nber of employees : 200
- Sponsor : Orange, PIAA, Virgin, Eurobet

TEST DRIVERS 2000

- Mark WEBER (AUS)

SUCCESSION OF DRIVERS 2000

- Petro de la ROSA : alls Grand Prix
- Jos VERSTAPPEN : alls Grand Prix

STATISTICS

- Number of Grand Prix : 354
- Number of victories : 0
- Number of pole-positions : 1
- Number of best laps during the race : 0
- Number of crivers' world titles : 0
- Number of constructors' titles : 0
- Total number of points scored : 164

POSITION IN WORLD CHAMPIONSHIP

1978 : 9th – 11 points	1990 : 9th – 2 points
1979 : 9th – 5 points	1991 : not classified
1980 : 7th – 11 points	1992 : 7th – 6 points
1981 : 8th – 10 points	1993 : 9th – 4 points
1982 : 10th – 5 points	1994 : 9th – 9 points
1983 : 10th – 4 points	1995 : 8th – 5 points
1984 : 9th – 6 points	1996 : 9th – 1 point
1985 : 8th – 14 points	1997 : 8th – 9 points
1986 : 10th – 1 points	1998 : 7th – 6 points
1987 : 6th – 11 points	1999 : 9th – 1 points
1988 : 4th – 23 points	2000 : 7th – 7 points
1989 : 7th – 13 points	

Egbhal Hamidy is the designer of the Arrows A21, the ultimate expression of aerodynamic efficiency. Throughout the year, the A21 was often the quickest car in a straight line. Hamidy's market value is bound to rise.

A pleasant surprise

«It's basically last year's Stewart car.» That was Jos Verstappen's perceptive description of this year's Arrows A21 after he tested his new mount for the first time last winter. Indeed, the A21 was the work of rising design star, Egbhal Hamidy, a refugee from the now defunct Stewart equipe. The Supertec engine was far better than any customer engine deserved to be. There is an old adage which says that the best way to make a small fortune out of Formula 1 is to start with a big one! No one understands this better than team principal Tom Walkinshaw. Immensely successful in racing and the motor industry in general, it would have been easy for the canny Scotsman to plough money from different ventures into his team, but losing money and making grands prix a hobby was never on the agenda. Instead, he has put several good deals in place, most noticeable to the media, the arrival of title sponsor Orange. The only unknown quantity for 2001 is what Walkinshaw will do with his Peugeot engines. They almost sunk the Prost team, but the Scotsman is made of sterner stuff than Alain Prost will no doubt galvanise his new partners and engine owners Asian Motor Technologies into getting their act together. This could be the dawning of a new era for the team which has been in Formula One longer than any other without a single grand prix win to its name.

Minardi-Fondmetal

20. Marc GENÉ

DRIVER PROFILE

- Name : GENÉ
- First names : Marc
- Nationality : Spanish
- Date of birth : March 29th 1974
- Place of birth : Sabadell (ESP)
- Lives in : Bellaterra (ESP)
- Marital status : single
- Kids : -
- Hobbies : reading, cinema & doing sports
- Favourite music : Dire Staits, rock & techno
- Favorite meal : pasta et paella
- Favourite drinks : milk
- Height : 173 cm
- Weight : 69 kg

STATISTICS

- Nber of Grand Prix : 31
- Victories : 0
- Pole-positions : 0
- Best laps : 0
- Accident/off : 4
- Not qualified : 0
- Laps in the lead : 0
- Km in the lead : 0
- Points scored : 1

PRIOR TO F1

1994-95 : British F3
1996 : 1st II Fisa Golden
    Cup Superformula
1997 : F3000
1998 : 1st Open Fortuna
    Nissan

F1 CAREER

1999 : Minardi / Ford. 1 point. 18th of championship.
2000 : Minardi / Fondmetal. 0 point.

21. Gaston MAZZACANE

DRIVER PROFILE

- Name : MAZZACANE
- First names : Gaston
- Nationality : Argentinian
- Date of birth : May 8, 1975
- Place of birth : La Plata (ARG)
- Lives in : La Plata (ARG)
- Marital status : single
- Kids : -
- Hobbies : strolling and shopping
- Favourite music : Bedondos, Red Hot Chili Peppers
- Favorite meal : asado (argentinain dish) and pasta
- Favourite drinks : orange juice and beer
- Height : 173 cm
- Weight : 68 kg

STATISTICS

- Nber of Grand Prix : 17
- Victories : 0
- Pole-positions : 0
- Best laps : 0
- Accident/off : 2
- Not qualified : 0
- Laps in the lead : 0
- Km in the lead : 0
- Points scored : 0

PRIOR TO F1

1994 : Champion F2000
    Italia
1999 : Minardit test driver

F1 CAREER

2000 : Minardi / Fondmetal. 0 point.

The second Spaniard on the grid has been one of the most impressive performers of the season. The problem is that when you drive a Minardi, you need a microscope to analyse that performance. Certainly, in terms of his own team he has out-qualified his team-mate fourteen times out of seventeen. When you consider the equipment he has to play with, he has probably got the most out of it, although we will never know, unless Michael Schumacher can be persuaded to try qualifying in a Minardi. Even though the team might have lost its Spanish backing for next year, Giancarlo Minardi still wants to hang on to his talented youngster. Nothing seems to dent his confidence and, a pleasant change for a grand prix driver, he makes stimulating and interesting conversation.

Nothing was expected of Gaston Mazzacane and nothing was delivered in return. The young Argentinian was clearly out of his depth: in Malaysian he qualified one and a half seconds slower than his team-mate. He was brought into the team by a sponsor but had never proved his worth in the lower formulae. He gradually withdrew into a shell as the season progressed, no doubt feeling he had to keep his head down. An uncertain future lies ahead.

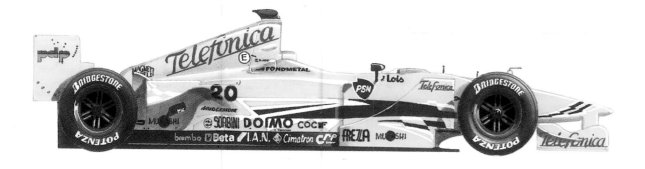

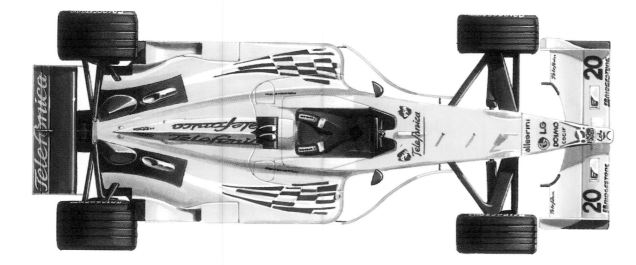

MINARDI-FONDMETAL M02
MARC GENÉ
AUSTRALIAN GRAND PRIX

Minardi-Ford M02

SPECIFICATION

- Chassis : *Minardi M 02*
- Engine : *Fond Metal V10*
- Tyres : *Bridgestone*
- Wheels : *Fondmetal*
- Fuel / oil : *Minardi*
- Brakes (discs) : *Carbone Industrie / Brembo*
- Brakes (calipers) : *Brembo*
- Transmission : *Minardi 6 gears, semi-autom.*
- Radiators : *Minardi*
- Plugs : *Champion*
- Shock absorbers : *Dynamics*
- Suspensions : *push rods (ft/bk)*
- Dry weight : *600 kg, including driver/camera*
- Wheelbase : *3030 mm*
- Front track : *1452 mm*
- Rear track : *1420.7 mm*

TEAM PROFILE

- Address : *Minardi Team SpA*
  Via Spallanzani 21
  48018 Faenza
  Italia
- Telephone : *(39) 0546 696 111*
- Fax : *(39) 0546 620 998*
- Web : *www.minardi.it*
- Established in : *1974*
- First Grand Prix : *Brazil 1985*
- Chairman : *Gabriele Rumi*
- General director : *Gabriele Rumi*
- Technical director : *Gustav Brunner*
- Chief mechanic : *Gabriele Pagliarini*
- Nber of employees : *140*
- Sponsors : *Fondmetal, Telefónica*

STATISTICS

- Number of Grand Prix : 254
- Number of victories : 0
- Number of pole-positions : 0
- Number of best laps during the race : 0
- Number of drivers' world titles : 0
- Number of constructors' titles : 0
- Total number of points scored : 28

Giancarlo Minardi has an uncanny ability to weather the storm. This year, Gabriele Rumi threw in the towel, handing over to the PSN group. Directors come and go, but Minardi is still there, a testimony to the original soul of the tiny team from Faenza.
▽

POSITION IN WORLD CHAMPIONSHIP

1985 : *not classified*	1993 : *8th – 7 points*
1986 : *not classified*	1994 : *10th – 5 points*
1987 : *not classified*	1995 : *10th – 1 point*
1988 : *10th – 1 point*	1996 : *not classified*
1989 : *10th – 6 points*	1997 : *not classified*
1990 : *not classified*	1998 : *not classified*
1991 : *7th – 6 points*	1999 : *10th – 1 point*
1992 : *11th – 1 point*	2000 : *not classified*

Waiting for better times to come

Minardi is diametrically opposed to the Sauber team. Underfinanced, run on a shoe-string, living from day to day, Giancarlo Minardi and the boys survive as the last of the true privateers on a diet of total enthusiasm, dedication and love of the sport. From the boss to the man who cooks the pasta, the Faenza boys and girls live, breathe and eat motor racing. This year, they could hold their heads up high thanks to a beautiful little car designed by the ever-enthusiastic Austrian, Gustav Brunner. The weakest point was the out-dated and underpowered Ford V10 engine. Despite this, qualifying within two or three seconds of a Ferrari, with less than a quarter of the budget is quite an achievement. As with all things Formula 1, the team's future depends on money. A new sponsor, in the shape of South American television company Panamerican Sports Network, might be the answer. On top of that, there are rumours that a Supertec V10 engine might be available, bringing with it a very welcome extra thirty to forty horsepower. That would be enough to make Giancarlo Minardi, Brunner and Gene a trio worth watching in 2001.

TEST DRIVERS 2000
- Fernando ALONSO (ESP)

SUCCESSION OF DRIVERS 2000

- Marc GENÉ : *alls Grand Prix*
- Gaston MAZZACANE : *alls Grand Prix*

Spotlight

To understand a Formula 1 season, it is necessary to approach it from several directions. That is why the "Formula 1 Yearbook" brings you the views of journalists from five different countries: Italy, England, Germany, Japan and Canada.

On a historical note, the first United States Grand Prix to be held at Indianapolis provided the excuse to look at the role played by the 500 Miles race in the F1 championship.

The Scuderia at the summit

2000 : punto di vista Italiano

by Christiano Chiavegato
«La Stampa»

In Japan, Ferrari finally succeeded in capturing the Drivers' World Championship. A masterpiece from Michael and the team saw the Prancing Horse standing on the Formula 1 summit. The groundwork had been done way back at the start of the season, when the German had pulled out a big lead over his rivals at McLaren. However, the route to the top was paved with misfortune: a broken suspension in Monaco after an exhaust split and overheated the component and two consecutive accidents at the start in Zeltweg and Hockenheim had thrown the series wide open again. Then successes in the Italian Grand Prix in Monza, followed by those at Indianapolis and Suzuka propelled the young man from Kerpen to the top of the leader board and out of reach of Mika Hakkinen's advances. It was party time in Maranello, in all of Italy and all over the world, wherever the tifosi gathered.

It was particularly satisfying for the president, Luca di Montezemolo and his general, Jean Todt, who had rebuilt the team, starting in 1991, when the former sporting director returned in a presidential role. Montezemolo had studied the problems in depth and after a few false starts, he found the man he was looking for, in the shape of the French manager; a great organiser with vast experience in all forms of motor sport, even if he had never worked in the Formula 1 arena. The master stroke was to take on the Englishman Ross Brawn to head up the technical team and South Africa's Rory Byrne as designer, both men having already won championships with Schumacher in their Benetton days. Todt's methods brought nothing but good, injecting the team with a sense of belonging, a sense of purpose, as well as discipline and method. Even missing out on the title by so little in 1997, 1998 and 1999 did nothing to dent the confidence and determination of the Ferrari men.

The concept and design of the F1-2000 was seen as an evolution of previous models. There was no risk taking with audacious technologies, even if the car was actually completely new. It turned out to be competitive on just about every type of circuit. The only exceptions were Magny Cours and Budapest, where the use of softer tyres had proved problematic and had created difficulties in maintaining the right temperature which led to excessive wear. Apart from that, the Scuderia posted just one engine failure, on Schumacher's car in France and two problems with hydraulic systems, which affected Barrichello, who was also knocked out of the Belgian race with a fuel pressure problem. These troubles aside, the car had proved remarkably

CHRISTIANO CHIAVEGATO, 59 years old, was introduced very young in journalism. He strated at "La Stampa" in 1959, while still attending various sporting events for "La Gazzetta dello Sport" for fifteen years. He has covered about ten Olympic Games, summer and winter, before concentring on motorsport at the end of the sixties. Since 1976, he has not missed a single GP and has written many books on Ferrari, and a biography of Niki Lauda.

reliable. Naturally, the car underwent several evolutions during the season, most of them positive. The one exception was a new front wing tried at Spa Francorchamps, where the delicate balance between suspension geometry and aerodynamics, compromised the settings on the demanding Ardennes circuit and had not provided the desired result.

Technically, it had been a good year and even the 049 engine underwent three development phases during the course of the championship. The final version, the 049C, played a significant part in securing pole position in the last few rounds, which served to put Schumacher in the most advantageous position possible.

While the team were celebrating in the Suzuka garage, in Fiorano, everyone was already hard at work.

It has to be said that the German did not always make the most of this and was often forced to give chase. Thanks to the race strategy devised by master tactician Ross Brawn, Michael almost always managed to make up for any lost time. These strategies were nowhere better demonstrated than at Indianapolis, when Formula 1

returned to the USA and one of the most famous circuits in the world, transformed from an oval to a mixed track. It was the setting for an extraordinary passing move on Coulthard and an emphatic one-two finish as Rubens Barrichello followed Michael home. In Japan, Hakkinen got off to a great start, but Ferrari's pit-stop strategy, combined with Schumacher's recovery in the decisive laps on a damp track turned the race into a triumph for the Italian team.

While the team were celebrating in the Suzuka garage, on the other side of the world in Fiorano and in the wind tunnel next to the Ferrari factory, everyone was already hard at work and looking to the future. For the past few months, Rory Byrne, who hardly ever comes to the races, especially now that he has become a father to son Sean, has already been working on a new car for 2001. *«Our plans are based on an evolution of the F1-2000, in terms of design,»* explained the South African. *«But it is evident that the new regulations, particularly as regards the need to improve the active safety elements on the car, will lead us to build a chassis with different dimensions. That involves a whole new study programme. As usual we have looked at all areas of the car. Our aim is to improve its balance, with better weight distribution. It's a never ending challenge. Whatever, we feel we have progressed, even if we know our rivals of the last few years will also react, as will other teams who are on the way up after a few less than great seasons. These days, the presence of so many of the top motor manufacturers has made it a tough fight with vast resources brought into play. Technology gets ever more sophisticated as do the materials used.»*

Jean Todt's plan is to keep the continuity going within the Gestione Sportiva. In theory, barring any last minute surprises, everyone is staying put. However, the number of people working on the Formula 1 programme has increased. The figure had already reached 550 people, out of a total of 1900 Ferrari employees, but since the end of 2000, the number increased to 600, with the creation of a new group, res-

ponsible for supplying engines to Prost and Sauber. A group of engineers and mechanics will work under the direction of Stefano Govoni to ensure the construction, development and maintenance of a hundred engines for the Swiss and French teams. Ferrari intends giving the maximum support to its customer teams.

The Maranello team will naturally concentrate on its own engines. Although working full time on the development of the 049C, Paolo Martinelli and his staff have been working on the new 050 power unit since last June. Without giving away any secrets, it is obvious that the engine for 2001 will constitute a major step forward when compared with the recent past. Several innovations have been studied, not just on the architecture of the engine, but also in terms of materials, electronics and the internals. It is no secret that the engineers are working on very innovative systems, concerning its distribution and weight reduction, as well as engine speed. One target which has tormented the designers all winter, concerns reducing consumption and increasing power. «At the same, we have concentrated on maintaining the reliability which has characterised these past few years, as one of Ferrari's main strengths,» says Martinelli. «It's an enormous challenge, which we have nevertheless tackled with great confidence after the results of the 2000 season. We know that the majority of the major motor manufacturers regard Formula 1 as a sales window which offers the best opportunity in terms of promoting the image of a marque. Our commitment is total.»

As for the chassis, Ross Brawn and Rory Byrne did not want to take too many risks. The 2001 Ferrari, code name 652, has not been designed as a completely different car to last season's, but is more of a natural evolution, based on all the data gathered from the circuits around the world, as well as all the testing data and figures obtained from the simulation rigs.

Its many fans have never abandoned the Prancing Horse, even in the most difficult times.

«Our task it to provide Michael and Rubens with a car which is competitive in all situations, easy to drive and set up,» explains the technical director. «The car should be quick and compliant, using aerodynamics which are both simple and functional. Over the years, we have learned that it is useless to go for over-complex solutions, even though our engineers leave no stone unturned. We also know that our opponents, both old and new will try all they can to beat us. But we are ready. The fact we have finally obtained our original goal has not affected our desire to go further. On the contrary, the championship which Michael has brought to Ferrari only serves to make us want to continue.»

Luca di Montezemolo, the President of Ferrari is counting on the technical strengths of the team and the solidarity created by Jean Todt, as well as the talents of the German champion and his Brazilian team mate. «The results are down to a group which we would like to keep unchanged,» he says. «They are all linked by a common denominator, a passion for Ferrari, which is unique in the world. We have been at the top level for several years and we did not always get what we deserved. We can only try to be the best. I would also like to recall the great difficulties we had to overcome and the criticism which often rained down on us. I often tell my colleagues that Ferrari would not be what it is without its critics. We are always a reference point, which is the destiny of the very best. We must not waver in our duty, which is to keep winning.»

The Scuderia has fought hard to turn round the barren years of the past and it is convinced it can keep the momentum it has acquired. Its many fans have never abandoned the Prancing Horse, even in the most difficult times. Now they are dreaming of another successful season. But they know it will not be easy. The fight is particularly tough, with several teams aiming for the championship. They are ready to fly their flags and do battle. In 2001, they will be the motivating force, spurring Ferrari on once again.

△

Winning both the drivers' and constructors' titles was down to a combination of factors, with Michael Schumacher just one, albeit vital element. It owed as much to the way Jean Todt had turned Ferrari into a crack fighting squad.

Michael Schumacher won his bet, bringing the drivers' crown back to Maranello after 21 barren years. Up against McLaren, he made the difference on the track at those crucial moments, transforming Ross Brawn's strategy into triumph.

▽

McLaren bite the dust

2000 : a British point of view

by Nigel Roebuck
«Autosport»

It was not until July that the 2000 Grand Prix season really began to come alive, and by that stage Bernie Ecclestone must have been getting a little nervous. Over time, both he and FIA President Max Mosley had frequently said how 'good for racing' it would be if Ferrari were to win the World Championship, but no one - least of all Bernie and Max - wanted to see Michael Schumacher clinch it by August. In the recent past, after all, as the TV Show has increasingly shoved aside the sport, we have grown accustomed to championship deciders at the final round.

Eight races in, though, with nine to go, Schumacher had five wins and a third place. With a Ferrari as reliable as ever, and much more competitive than before, Michael led by 22 points, and looked to have the thing comfortably won. To some degree, he had had it easy. Mika Hakkinen, for example, took pole position in the first three races, and should certainly have won the first two, in Australia and Brazil; as it was, he finished in neither - engine failures each time - and Schumacher scooped up both. Then, at Imola, Mika held off Michael until an electronic glitch cut his engine momentarily, which reduced his lead, which in turn allowed the Ferrari to get in front at the second stops. It was then nip-and-tuck to the flag, but passing at Imola is nigh impossibile; thus, Schumacher made it three on the trot.

By common consent, at this he is the best, the man who inherited Ayrton Senna's mantle as the natural pole-sitter

---

Jackie Stewart has said that, no matter who you are, winning a World Championship means that you start the following season with a certain lack of...something, be it motivation, zest, hard edge, whatever. «*Look down the years, and you'll see that not too many drivers have won it two years running. Mika did, and it was a remarkable achievement, but maybe now it's caught up with him...*»

Maybe it had. Although Hakkinen won the Spanish Grand Prix, it was only after pit stop problems had taken Schumacher from the lead, and thereafter Mika was plainly been off his game for a while. Nowhere was this more apparent than in qualifying. By common consent, at this he is the best, the man who inherited Ayrton Senna's mantle as the natural pole-sitter, the one who could always find that extra tenth in the dying minutes of a session. Towards mid-season, though, Hakkinen went three straight races without making the front row. Unheard of. All kinds of theories were put forward, one of which was that Mika was preoccupied by thoughts of imminent fatherhood, and was not concentrating on his racing as previously he always had.

Hakkinen's manager, Keke Rosberg, laughed at

that. «*Listen, Mika is delighted that Erja is pregnant, but he's also completely relaxed about it. If he's a little off form at the moment, it has nothing to do with that, believe me. There's nothing fundamentally wrong with Mika - nothing that a holiday wouldn't put right. To be honest, I think he's tired - as simple as that. Think about it: he has won the World Championship for the last two years, and each time he has to do it at the last race. Over a long period of time, he's been under a tremendous amount of pressure, and although he handles pressure better than anyone - certainly better than Schumacher - I think it has caught up with him. If you ask me, all he needs is a few days away from his job, away from testing, away from PR work.*»

As Hakkinen's star temporarily fell, so David Coulthard's moved in the opposite direction. Indeed, since the 'plane crash survived in early May by David and his American fiancee Heidi, he seemed more relaxed, more at peace with himself, than at any time before. To come through an experience of that kind had to change your perspective of life, to define very sharply what mattered, and what did not. The impression was that DC had become less intense about his motor racing - and that his driving had benefitted. There was a formidably insouciant

quality about him now which was never there before. He finished second in Spain only five days after the accident; afterwards it emerged that he had raced with three broken ribs. Coulthard had won at Silverstone and Monte Carlo, and if his performances had perhaps been flattered by his team mate's loss of form, so he seemed consistently a more potent force than before. In Montreal he gave Schumacher all he could handle in the early laps. until an unfortunate stop/go penalty effectively ended the race right there.

Soon after half-season, though, Michael's fortunes began to unravel. In the first eight races, he had failed to finish once, at Monaco, and that, given Ferrari's extraordinary reliability, might have been expected to be his lot for the year. At Magny-Cours, though, he had an engine failure - and that after being squarely out-duelled by an inspired Coulthard. That truly was DC's day of days. In France he looked like the driver he had always threatened to be, so that, as he chased Schumacher, you simply knew that on this afternoon he was not going to be denied. Michael, in his usual way, tried to intimidate him, edging him off the road as he got alongside, but on the next lap David passed him, and that was the end of it. Next, it was Hakkinen's turn to close on the Ferrari, but somehow Mika's pursuit was far less convincing, and although he eventually finished second to his team mate (after Schumacher's retirement), there were few doubts in people's minds that, at least for the moment, Coulthard had taken over as McLaren's *de facto* number one driver.

It didn't last. After Magny-Cours, Ron Dennis told Hakkinen he was to do nothing until the next race, in Austria; he was to stay home in Monaco, spend time with his wife and friends, relax. For now, all the testing would be done by

NIGEL ROEBUCK, 53 years old, decided to quit his industrial job and enter journalism at the age of 24. In 1971, he starts writing for the American magazine «Car & Driver», before joining the British weekly motor racing magazine «Autosport» in 1976. He is covering Formula One since 1977, while workingfor the «Sunday Tmes», for the «Auto Week» and the Japanese magazine «Racing On».

Coulthard and Olivier Panis. In the opinion of many McLaren people, Panis's contribution to the team over the year could scarcely be over-estimated. Olivier had left the Prost team at the end of 1999, his career in some disarray. « It was a difficult time, » he said, « but then Keke Rosberg and Didier Cotton took over my management, and working with them has changed my life completely, and not only in terms of my mentality; they organise everything for me, leaving me to concentrate on driving. »

It was Rosberg and Cotton who suggested that Panis should temporarily set racing aside, and become McLaren's test driver. Olivier agreed at once. « One hundred per cent! Yes, OK. I want to race, but what attracted me was the idea of working for McLaren, the best team, and of establishing my level of performance against the regular drivers. The team is unbelievable. I never see any pressure inside McLaren. The attitude is, 'OK, we know the problem - now we work logically until we solve it. There is no fighting - I never hear the volume up. Never! Everything is clever; everything is true. But it's logic, not magic. »

While Hakkinen relaxed at home, between the French and Austrian Grands Prix, Panis pounded round Mugello, in four days covering more than 2250 kms - the equivalent of seven Grands Prix.

At the A1-Ring Mika was duly back to his very best, taking pole position and dominating the race, with Coulthard second. Better yet, for the McLaren drivers' World Championship aspirations, was that Schumacher was eliminated in a first corner shunt - and the same was to happen at Hockenheim, where Hakkinen have also have won, had not the lunatic in the plastic raincoat brought out the Safety Car, which wiped away Mika's considerable lead. Through all this, Schumacher's championship lead held out, but barely; he had 56 points, with both the McLaren boys on 54. Never mind, put the recent past behind you, hold your nerve. In Hungary he took pole position consummately, and, with McLaren apparently unable to balance their cars

properly, must have expected the winning to start again. Wrong. Hakkinen got away brilliantly, dived to the inside of the Ferrari at the first corner, and left Schumacher with no choice but to cede. Thereafter, his car now working to perfection, he drove away.

If Michael looked shocked at the Hungaroring, at Spa he seemed almost resigned. In the late laps, Mika hunted him down, refused to be intimidated by a ruthless chop at over 190mph, and passed him into Les Combes in one of the great manouevres of F1 history. This, beyond doubt, was the victory of the season.

Just as a memorable fight seemed in prospect, there was smoke, then flame, from the Mercedes V10

Now, suddenly, Hakkinen had a six-point lead over Schumacher, with four races to go, and looked set to take his third champion-ship on the trot.

Schumacher, meantime, grimly said he knew what he had to do. And he did it, too. At Monza, Ferrari were miraculously quicker than expected, and Michael beat Mika with ease. This was a weekend when McLaren never really got themselves together - indeed, Hakkinen said he was agreeably surprised to finish second in an ill-handling car.

«This was our fault, not Mika's,» Dennis commented. «For some reason, we simply haven't operated well as a team this weekend.» The real turning point, though, was Indianapolis. Towards the halfway point, Hakkinen was closing on Schumacher as he had at Spa, but just as a memorable fight seemed in prospect, there was smoke, then flame, from the Mercedes V10. As at Melbourne, as at Interlagos, Mika was out with engine failure, leaving Michael a canter to the flag. Now eight points to the good again, Michael knew that two second places at Suzuka and Sepang - even if Mika were to win both races - would be enough for the title. In the past, many drivers in that situation have quite deliberately gone 'for points', but Schumacher is not like that, and in Japan drove out of his skin to keep in touch with an equally brilliant Hakkinen. A little drizzle was all it took. On a treacherous surface, the Ferrari closed on the McLaren, then got the better of it at the

last stops. Michael had his third victory in a month, and with it his third title. Ifs and buts. If Hakkinen hadn't been robbed of the first two races, hadn't perhaps subconsciously begun to wonder if the title was already lost, the mental weariness in June might have hit less hard; if Coulthard, quite brilliant in the same period, had managed to sustain that form, two McLarens, rather than one, would have been able to pressure Schumacher... The fact is, though, that over the whole season Michael did a better job than anyone else. And as well as that, of course, he is in a team which revolves around him. No one in the business calls a race as Ross Brawn does, and down the years Jean Todt's most significant achievement has been to pull the disparate strings of Ferrari together, to « organise » the team as it never was before. There is a discipline at Maranello these days that once would have been unthinkable, and Schumacher, Brawn and Todt have all played their part in instilling it. If just one of these three were to leave, one feels, the spell would be broken.

As in '98 and '99, Schumacher and Hakkinen were the dominant players in the World Championship. They may have had their individual glitches in 2000, but at Suzuka, as at so many races this year, they had the place to themselves. Before the start, Coulthard, third on the grid, talked of having the best seat in the house, but one lap in he had no view at all: Mika and Michael were gone. In Japan the degree of superiority exerted by the two heavyweights of the modern era was startling. DC and Rubens Barrichello, finished third and fourth, but well over a minute adrift. While each has had his moments of glory this season, even occasionally had a slight edge over his number one, the fact is that week in, week out, Schumacher and Hakkinen are on a different level. « Congratulations to Michael, » Ron Dennis said in Japan. « He's done a very good job - but we'll get the championship back next year... » Don't bet against it.

△
After a difficult start to the season, Mika Hakkinen went on to regain the upper hand over David Coulthard. Once again, he proved he was the only man capable of challenging Michael Schumacher for the title.

△
Lack of reliability from Mercedes cost Mika Hakkinen dear at the very worst moment. An engine on fire during the grand prix at Indianapolis proved to be one of the key moments of the 2000 season, opening the door to the titles for Schumacher and Ferrari.

◁
While the dream of taking three consecutive titles eluded Mika Hakkinen, the Finn can take comfort from the fact that, in 2000, he was yet again one of the two best drivers in the world, the other being Michael Schumacher.

Michael will never be Boris

2000 aus deutscher Sicht

by Anno Hecker
«Frankfurter Allgemeine Zeitung»

Zurich at the beginning of July: Germany has just won the right to stage the 2006 World Cup and a wave of joy sweeps the country, after the disastrous performance from the national side in the European Championship in Belgium and Holland. Once again, Beckenbauer was in charge of the team and even Michael Schumacher was very impressed when he met «The Kaiser» a few days later, during a charity match in Rome. *«He has great presence.»* Maybe that is the small but subtle difference between the immoveable institution that is Beckenbauer and the Formula 1 star that is the ever controversial Schumacher; one the Messiah of German football, the other the God of motor racing.

They were all there for the European Grand Prix at the Nurburgring in May: the showbiz and sports personalities, the major political figures led by German chancellor Gerhard Schroder and the President of the European Union, Romano Prodi. The movers and shakers had realised that Formula 1 was a good backdrop for self-publicity.

Neither Schroder nor Prodi had shown any previous interest in motor racing. But Schumacher has rekindled German interest in Formula 1. There are four Germans in the sport and two constructors have invested money and motors, while German sponsors invest millions. And all that because a man of humble origins is so successful.

«I never said it would be easy. Whatever happens, I will fight to the end.»

More than any of his fellow countrymen, he has accelerated a boom every bit as rapid as a Formula 1 car. The bad behaviour of the soccer stars who had failed to score a single point during the European championship was the subject on everyone's lips and the politicians were worried about the reputation of the country, based on its excellence at soccer, ever since Becker and Graf had packed away their tennis rackets. The country's most famous athlete, Dieter Baumann was involved in a drugs scandal, and there was German boxing champion who actually came from Poland. It seemed that only Schumacher was set fair on the path to success that summer with his Ferrari, even

if Mika Hakkinen's crushing form was a worry for the fans. *«I never said it would be easy,»* said Schumacher in Hockenheim at the end of July. *«Whatever happens, I will fight to the end.»* Those comments went down well with the fans. He encapsulates, at least when seen from the outside, the German values of application, discipline and availability. Therefore, that summer, Schumacher was the only German sports

star in action and he had given a new coat of polish to the weakened «made in Germany» tag.

However, although he is portrayed as a knight on a white charger, without fault or blame, before his championship win, Schumacher was not seen as being on the same level as Becker or Beckenbauer. These two men have a great standing in the country and not just with the masses. Even the intellectuals discuss the merits of their footballing hero, with the tennis star being accorded similar status. Schumacher however, has split the country in two. On the one hand there are his fans who will not hear him criticised, while others attack his every move both on and off the track. Since his collision with Jacques Villeneuve

in the final round of the 1997 championship, he has been tagged with a reputation for being a bad loser, even in Germany. After the Jerez incident, a journalist from Frankfurt even tried to have him brought to court to answer charges of attempted murder. The move was thrown out, but the accusations linger. An independent market research company found that German rejected the concept of national pride and when asked to pick the most popular Formula 1 driver, Mika Hakkinen emerged at the top of the list. That might have something to do with Mercedes amusing television commercials featuring the Finn. Even Schumacher admitted they were effective. *«They make Mika seem like a fantastic guy, but I am not sure if he really is that way.»*

So what is Schumacher really like? His image, even in his homeland, is far from clear, as little is known about him, neither his work nor his private life. Everyone could see the elegance of a Beckenbauer or spot the pain in Becker's eyes when defeat stared him in the face or the evident pleasure he took in winning. But Schumacher's art, alone in the cockpit of his car, means it is hard to see his anger, irritation, joy or disappointment, hidden behind his visor. The only image is of a German winning race after race in a calculated and humourless manner. Typically Schumacher, typically German. *«I am not a computer,»* declared the Ferrari star, slightly irritated when being quizzed as to his strengths. The 31 year old driver certainly has the ability to reel off all the laps of a race with metronomic precision. Everything come down to just tenths of a second. That is why, when fighting with his rivals, he seems to be constantly thinking and not just driving. *«Of course you have to have the*

ANNO HECKER, 36 years old, worked first as a physical education instructor befor turning to journalism in 1986. After working as a political correspondent for a Bonn news agency, he joined "Frankfurter Allgemeine Zeitung" in 1991 to cover motor sports. He specialised in stories combinig politics and sport.

talent. *But without a lot of hard work, you cannot do anything,»* he explains. During 2000, as every year, he was pushed to his limits by the desire to be the absolute best and to become the first driver since Jody Scheckter in 1979 to win the world championship at the wheel of a Ferrari. But in some ways, his desire for perfection is also the expression of a certain lack of confidence, which despite attempts to hide it, would show through in the early days of his career. He would look tense in public. He was always immaculately turned out and even on the hottest of days, his race suit would be zipped up to the top. The world had to see an unassailable Schumacher in the mould of the Mercedes school.

In Formula 1, that respect is accorded to those who win and earn a lot of money.

He was also seen as an excellent driver and a young man who was driven by a taste for success which had alienated him from others. There was no trace of the easy charm of Beckenbauer or the rebellious nature of Becker. But Schumacher lives in Switzerland now and has no desire to become his country's favourite son. *«I just want to be respected, nothing more, nothing less.»* In Formula 1, that respect is accorded to those who win and earn a lot of money. It is a simple scale to quantify. Schumacher acts according to this ideal as it sets the hierarchy in his world. His calculations are based on human and mechanical capital. It is particularly evident when his results are compared with those of Hakkinen and Coulthard. This summer, Schumacher defended himself fiercely against

accusations that he did not regard the Scot as a serious rival for the world championship, even when Coulthard was second ahead of Schumacher. *«If you look at the last 15 races, one can see that Hakkinen is quicker I cannot change my judgement based on just a couple of races. Yes, Coulthard won in Monaco, but anyone looking at Hakkinen's times can see what happened.»* Schumacher likes to consider all the facts. He trusts figures and data when it comes to analysing his rivals, which can be dangerous. Driver and team statistics are not something he bothers with. He regards them as a simple accumulation dating back to a past that has no bearing on the present. *«Maybe they will become important when I am old and will tell stories to my grandchildren. History does not interest me.»* That is why he has also been unable to satisfy the demands of the Ferrari fans the first time he stood on the podium. Up until the Italian Grand Prix, this was an accurate assessment in that their admiration for him was based entirely on the results he delivered. Even Ferrari President Montezemolo regarded him as a ghost driver, because of his inability to communicate in Italian, since when Schumacher began taking Italian lesson. The result was that, at the pre-season launch this year, he greeted the crowd in their own tongue, even if there was the odd error. The final bouquet came in Japan, when asked to say a few words in his own language in the TV press conference, he chose to utter a few thank yous in Italian. It translated as: *«this is the best moment of my life. I thank all the team, thank you, thank you, thank you.»* If this had been planned, then at least it had been planned with the best of intentions. Then there was the famous moment in Monza, when Schumacher allowed his emotions to escape. For the first time in ten years, he totally lost all self-control, weeping and sobbing in front of the cameras, having been overcome with emotion after winning in front of the tifosi. He had beaten McLaren and Hakkinen and it seemed like a turning point in the championship.
The enthusiasm of the sea of red fans below the podium and being asked what it felt like to equal the number of wins of the late Ayrton Senna, proved too much. *«It was a mixture*

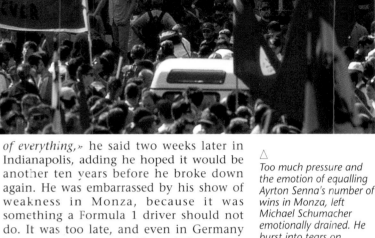

of everything,» he said two weeks later in Indianapolis, adding he hoped it would be another ten years before he broke down again. He was embarrassed by his show of weakness in Monza, because it was something a Formula 1 driver should not do. It was too late, and even in Germany his strongest critics could not believe their eyes. *«The most surprising reaction is that people now regard me as a human being, when I always thought I was one,»* he declared.

He absorbs all information relating to his car like a sponge.

His private life is just that and we can only guess at what sort of father he is, although there is always a sparkle in his eyes when he talks of his children Gina-Maria and Mick. His family is what he loves most. His future is also a secret as he does not like looking further ahead than his career as a driver. He absorbs all information relating to his car like a sponge. Already, back in his Benetton days, his brilliant ideas had got him out of the odd scrape. *«Once at a test, Michael remembered something we had tried over a year ago and instantly went quicker,»* recalled Ross Brawn who was with him then as he is now. His intelligence has also allowed him to learn to speak impeccable English and he speaks the language of F1 almost better than he does German. In his mother tongue, Schumacher tries to impress by using rhetoric, but he rarely trips over his words. But what can one expect from someone who hardly ever reads newspapers or books to discover the world outside the paddock. *«I am interested in all sorts of things. But at the moment, I have no time to follow them up,»* he said back in March. *«I want to be world champion with Ferrari.»* He has managed to do even more than that. The chancellor immediately sent a congratulatory telegram to Suzuka, entire television programmes were devoted to him and newspapers from both ends of the German political spectrum paid hommage. They raised him to the level of a Beckenbauer and a Becker. His championship win was mainly to blame, but he had lit the spark with his show of emotion in Monza.

△
Too much pressure and the emotion of equalling Ayrton Senna's number of wins in Monza, left Michael Schumacher emotionally drained. He burst into tears on television. It was one of the rare moments when the German proved he is human after all.

◁
He had waited five years, since leaving Benetton and his two previous championship titles, but finally he brought the winner's laurels to Ferrari. He had conquered the greatest challenge of his career, which gave him plenty to smile about.

Atmosphere

If people are prepared to leave the comfort of their armchairs to travel to the race track in such large numbers, the main attraction has to be the atmosphere. It's a question of the senses, smelling and hearing the cars to appreciate the speed and the noise.
It is difficult to convey these many sensations on paper. The nearest one can do is to concentrate on a few subjects and allow them to express themselves.

Formula Flirt

Legend has it that the Formula 1 paddocks are crammed with charming creatures. Sadly these days, that is far from the truth. Nevertheless, you can always trust the photographers to flush out any pretty girls who might just keep the legend alive.

ATMOSPHERE

Modern impressionists

Harmony of form and colour represented in bodywork and its reflection. Some choice images to feast your eyes on.

ATMOSPHERE

Waiting for Honda

After pride follows the fall. Having finished third in the 1999 Constructors' Championship, picking up two wins along the way, the Jordan team dropped to sixth in 2000 with only one real podium finish for third place in Indianapolis.

Never mind. The yellow team is keeping the faith and is hoping for better things in 2001 when a works Honda engine, just like Jacques Villeneuve's, augurs well for the future.

ATMOSPHERE

And the gravel flies!

Driving a Formula 1 car is all about finding its limits. The easiest way to do that is to exceed them, which often entails a quick trip into the gravel trap.

ATMOSPHERE

A votre santé

After the effort of racing, the podium ceremony gives the drivers a chance to let off the steam they have accumulated over 300 kilometres. A Bridgestone cap pulled down tight, a bottle of Champagne in hand is deliverance F1 style. Mumm, the Winner's Champagne.

ATMOSPHERE

One to forget

The Prost Grand Prix team had a terrible 2000 season. It divorced its engine supplier after an acrimonious squabble and a strike by the Peugeot crew in Magny Cours. Sponsors left and it took all summer to negotiate a new engine supply. Just about everything went wrong for Alain Prost and his French team. Looking forward to 2001 and Ferrari power.

ATMOSPHERE

ATMOSPHERE

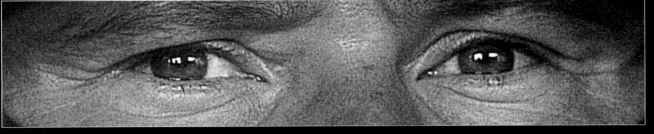

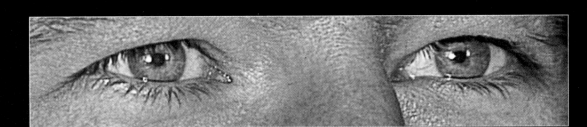

Mind those shades

Without their helmets, the Formula 1 drivers are hard to recognise, except for the true fans. Are you one?

(left page, from top to bottom)

Mika Hakkinen, Jos Verstappen, Michael Schumacher, Nick Heidfeld, Johnny Herbert, Jenson Button, David Coulthard.

(right page from top to bottom)

Jacques Villeneuve, Eddie Irvine, Jean Alesi, Jarno Trulli, Pedro Diniz, Alexander Wurz.

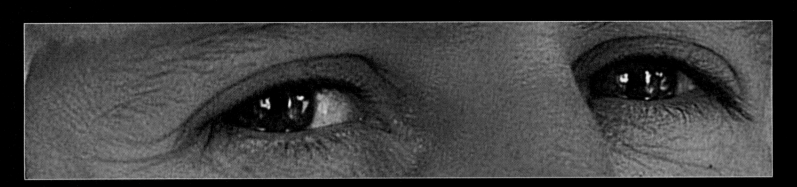

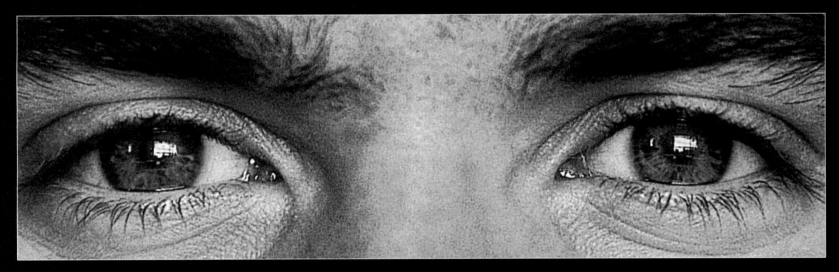

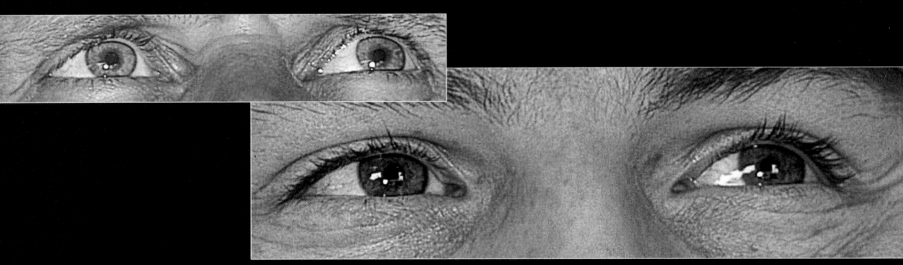

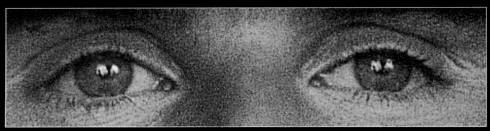

ATMOSPHERE

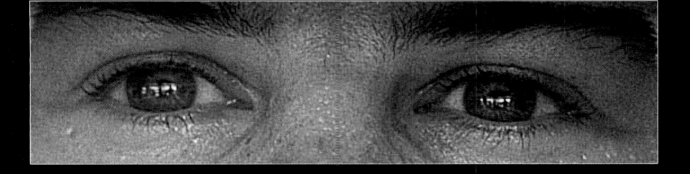

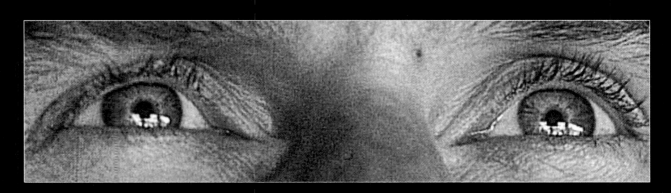

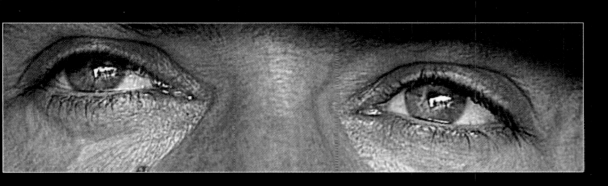

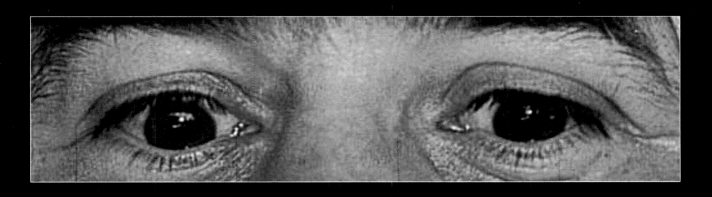

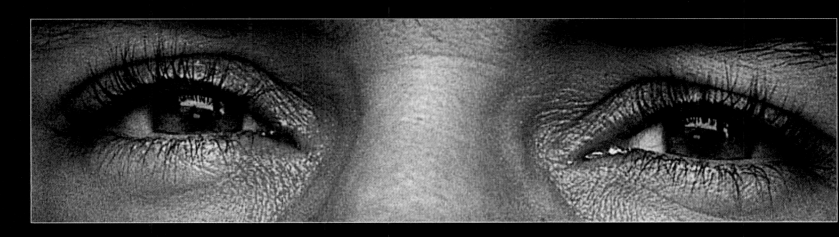

ATMOSPHERE

The 17 GPs

Once the season had kicked off in Australia, the grands prix followed one another in relentless fashion. A race a fortnight, without any respite, meant the F1 folk criscrossed the ocean in all directions.

From Melbourne to Sepang, the season was played out in 17 varied episodes, reflected in these images.

Red Letter Day

There's nothing like a one-two finish to kick off a Formula 1 season instyle!

For the first time in five years, Ferrari appeared to have emerged fromwinter testing with all guns blazing. Usually the Scuderia would turn up inAustralia only to give away a second a lap to the McLarens, before workingflat out to make up the deficit. 2000 would see this unhealthy traditionbroken at last. Having said that, both McLarens were also very competitive on Australian soil. It looked like being another season-long battle if thered cars were finally to lift the drivers' title.

QANTAS AUSTRALIAN GRAND PRIX
MELBOURNE

QANTAS AUSTRALIAN GRAND PRIX

Starring role

Zooming in on Rubens Barrichello (top.) Jacques Villeneuve (centre) and Mika Hakkinen (below.) All three were stars at this Australian Grand Prix.

The first grand prix saw the little Brazilian make it to the podium in second place, having briefly led the race.

As for the Canadian, he scored his first points for two years and the BAR team's first ever points. It was a breath of fresh air after a difficult first season.

The Finn was the hero of qualifying, with yet another pole position to his name, the 22nd of his career. In the race, the reigning world champion led for a few laps before retiring on lap 19. Victory will come later.

QANTAS AUSTRALIAN GRAND PRIX

Suspense in Interlagos

Night had fallen at the Interlagos circuit, but work was still going on in the garage used by the scrutineers. And there was a lot to do.

A few hours earlier, Michael Schumacher had won the Brazilian Grand Prix ahead of David Coulthard and Giancarlo Fisichella. This was not the end of it, because the track in Brazil had proved to be very bumpy this year, having recently been resurfaced! As a consequence, the cars had suffered and taken a pounding.

During the course of post-race scrutineering, the FIA felt that all the points scoring cars, with the exception of Fisichella's Benetton, did not comply with the regulations. Finally, after several agonising hours, all of them were declared legal with the exception of David Coulthard's McLaren, which was disqualified.

**GRANDE PRÊMIO DO BRASIL
INTERLAGOS**

Hat-trick!

Michael Schumacher's insolent domination of the championship continued in Imola, where the German racked up his third win on the trot.

However, once again, it was Mika Hakkinen who was quickest in qualifying, also for the third time in three races. Unfortunately, just as he had done in the previous two rounds, the Finn, having made a good start, ran into unexpected problems. This time it was debris on the track and a most unwelcome Mercedes engine cut out which lasted a mere two thousandths of a second.

Michael Schumacher did not need to be asked twice to claim another victory. In 2000 a trend was clearly emerging, in that it only took a tiny slip up from one of the two top teams, for the other to profit.

RAN PRÊMIO WARSTEINER DI SAN MARINO
IMOLA

 **GRAN PREMIO WARSTEINER DI SAN MARINO**

The magic of Formula 1 expressed in componentry. In an era when electronics have the upper hand and the chassis are masterpieces of carbon fibre, it is sweet to see that the old skills have not died and good old aluminium can still be fashioned, just like in the good old days.

Welcome to Silverstone

"The Home of British Motor Racing" says the sign over the main entrance to Silverstone. As things turned out, home is just where most spectators who turned up on Friday wanted to be and as for the next day, the organisers actually warned them to stay at home rather than risk the notorious Northamptonshire car parks. Both days of practice were marked by incredibly heavy storms, although a miracle on Sunday saw the rains stay away for the race.

The rain had been falling for several weeks beforehand and turned the car parks into such a swamp that the organisers had to close them on Saturday. Sunday was not much better. It took so long to pull the cars into the car parks that ten mile queues were forming outside.

Those who fought through the mud in time to see the race were rewarded with a British victory, courtesy of David Coulthard who took his seventh Formula 1 career win.

FOSTER'S BRITISH GRAND PRIX
SILVERSTONE

Mika's counter attack

With three consecutive wins under his belt, it seemed that Michael Schumacher already had the championship sewn up. This premise did not take into account the qualities of the McLaren MP4/15, which had failed to capitalise on the enormous potential it had so clearly demonstrated. This situation could not go on for ever. The people at Mercedes were praying that the gremlins which had affected them since the start of the year would soon switch camps. In Barcelona they got their wish. Having started in the lead, Michael Schumacher had a fourth win within his grasp. But this time fate intervened. A mistake by his team during the pit stops was followed by a slow puncture. These two glitches were enough to relegate him to fifth, while Mika Hakkinen won the day. Suspense had returned to the championship.

GRAN PRÊMIO MARLBORO DE ESPAÑA
BARCELONE

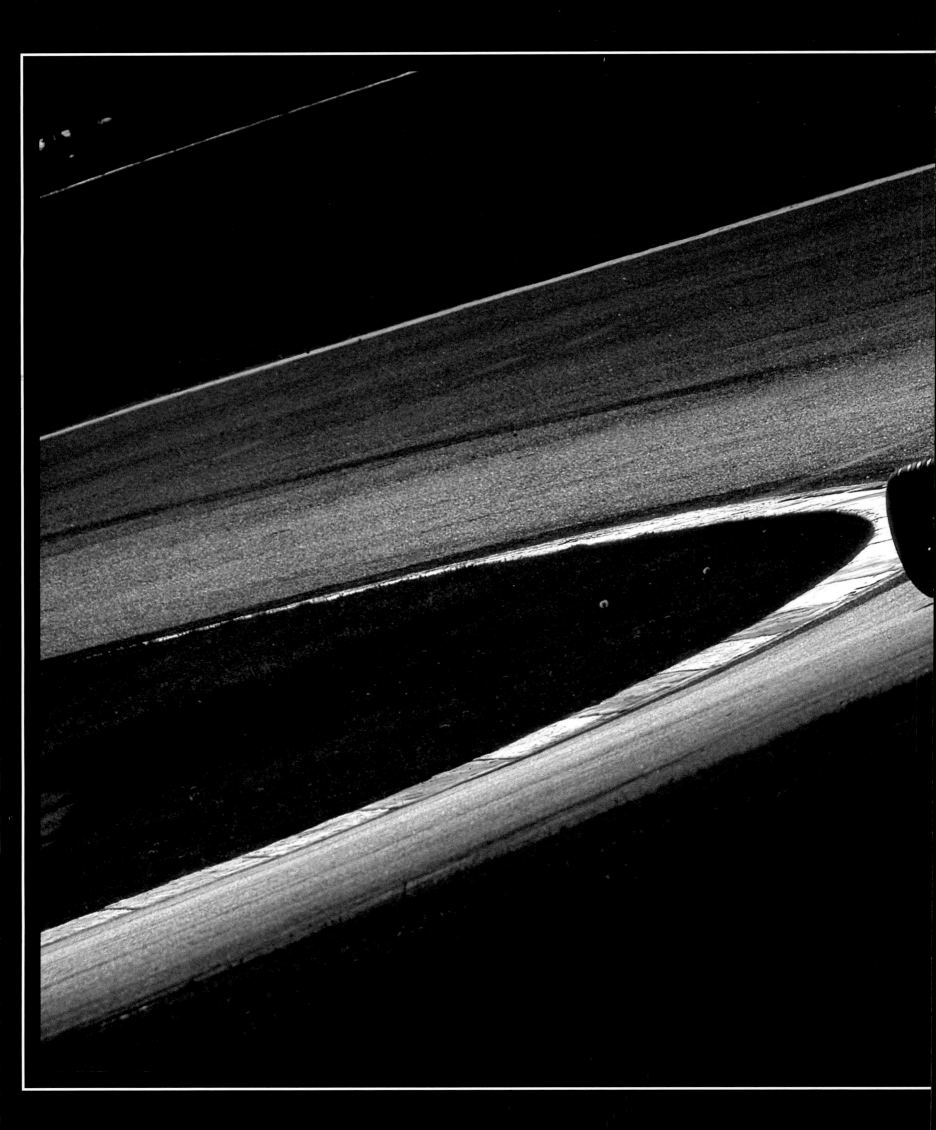

 **GRAN PREMIO MARLBORO DE ESPAÑA**

The Prost team in silhouette at the Barcelona circuit. With Jean Alesi 8th and Nick Heidfeld 20th, it was another dog day afternoon for the Prost-Peugeot boys in Saturday's qualifying. On Sunday, the Frenchman crashed out of the race and the German finished, albeit in sixteenth place.

GRAN PREMIO MARLBORO DE ESPAÑA

Schumi at home

Michael Schumacher never ceases to amaze. Not that the German's victory constituted a surprise. Ever since he came into Formula 1 back in 1991, the resident of Vufflens-le-Chateau has always shown himself to be completely at ease in the rain. The downpour which fell on the Nurburgring circuit could not have arrived at a better time to show off his talent. What is surprising is the eternally youthful enthusiasm he shows after a win, even when it is his thirty ninth.

If the track had remained dry, Schumacher might have faced a more difficult task. Because, yet again, the European Grand Prix suggested that in performance terms the Ferrari was just a notch under the McLaren. However, once again, the Ferrari man came out on top, making the most of the conditions.

WARSTEINER GRAND PRIX OF EUROPE
NÜRBURGRING

 **WARSTEINER GRAND PRIX OF EUROPE**

There is no point in starting from pole if you don't leave on time. No doubt the tortoise might have explained this to the hare if he knew anything about Formula 1. David Coulthard had qualified ahead of the rest but he was overtaken by Mika Hakkinen and Michael Schumacher as soon as the red lights went out. He would finish on the third rung of the podium.

WARSTEINER GRAND PRIX OF EUROPE

The star of David

Does David Coulthard have a guiding star looking over him? Until now, the Scotsman had always been considered a handy journeyman driver, but a definite step below the likes of Mika Hakkinen, Michael Schumacher, Jacques Villeneuve and even Heinz-Harald Frentzen.

But suddenly, since his plane crash on 2nd May, the man known by his initials "DC" seemed to have become a man transformed. For the first time in two years, he had out-qualified Mika Hakkinen, at the European Grand Prix. In Monaco, he did it again, lining up third on the grid while the Finn was down in fifth place.

In the race, while Hakkinen lost his way with brake and gearbox problems, David Coulthard swept into the lead and won the Monaco Grand Prix. It has to be said though that he profited from Michael Schumacher's exhaust problems, as the German had led for most of the race.

GRAND PRIX DE MONACO
MONTE-CARLO

The German had been testing in Fiorano on the Friday.

Michael Schumacher on pole - it's a dream

Every year, the Monaco Grand Prix hosts another round of the battle of the barriers. For the drivers, the 78 race laps consist above all of avoiding contact with the infamous metal barriers which line the entire circuit.
In order to avoid them, at an average speed of 150 km/h, you must stay calm and therefore, under no circumstances try and overtake. At Monaco, there is simply nowhere to attempt this sort of manoeuvre.
Therefore, securing pole in the Principality is a good part of winning the race. On Saturday, Michael Schumacher was regal in the way he took pole and tucked it out of harms way in his pocket. As for the start, he was counting on getting that right too. While other drivers enjoyed the traditional Friday rest day, Michael helicoptered to Ferrari's Fiorano track to practice the delicate art of race starts. *"On our car, the procedure that has to be followed at the start is quite complicated,"* admit-

ted Schumacher. *"It has often caused us problems at the start, but I think that now we have found a satisfactory solution to our problems."*
On Saturday at any rate, the German did not stint himself, pulling out a comfortable advantage over his rivals. *"I have to admit everything was perfect today,"* rejoiced Schumacher after qualifying. *"It's like a dream, but I have to keep my feet on the ground. The reality is that this will be a very long race and I will have to make a good start to stand a chance of winning."* While Michael Schumacher got it all right on the day, Mika Hakkinen got it all wrong. Fifth on

the grid, his every attempt was thwarted by some sort of problem. *"Of course this is not the grid position I wanted,"* he complained. *"In Monaco, you can lose a lot of time if you are not in the right place at the right time. Every time I went out, I was caught out by yellow flags or slower cars. It was as though they were waiting for me."*
Mika Hakkinen no doubt regretted not having gone for a time during the first half hour of the session when, to the great disappointment of the spectators, the track was completely deserted.

"Get in the car please." Jarno Trulli prepares to take part in a qualifying session which will see him land a place on the front row of the grid.

Trulli surprising

"To be honest I didn't expect to be here." During the post-qualifying press conference, Jarno Trulli could not hide his surprise, but he relaxed into the role of front row runner. *"I thought I might be able to get onto one of the first three rows, but not right at the front! Up until now, we have had a lot of problems since Thursday, so it's hard to believe. We had to completely change my front suspension which wasn't working and I started from scratch this morning. It's almost a miracle that everything worked out fine."*
Second place for the Italian, combined with the fourth spot for team-mate Heinz-Harald Frentzen certainly proved that the Jordan Mugen-Hondas were on form on this twisty track. *"Yes, I think our chassis works better on this type of circuit than on the fast tracks. But we also have a new version of the Mugen-Honda engine which is a real step forward."* As for victory, the Italian preferred not to think about it. *"I don't think I can win here,"* he admitted. *"Maybe I can finish on the podium, but no better. I still have a few small worries about the car which we will try and fix between now and the race."*
The Monaco Grand Prix could often be as dull as a Sunday afternoon drive, but it could also throw up some astonishing surprises.

A symphony of colour and noise. The printed page cannot convey the atmosphere and sound which reigns over the Principality during the grand prix weekend, but it can hint at the majesty of the setting, the azure blue of the sky and the nonchalant way the boats float on the harbour. No contest, it is the best race setting of the season.

Jarno Trulli certainly looked well placed to profit from any mistake if Michael Schumacher got it wrong at the start.

The jewel of the season

Every year, on the first day of practice, when one sees the cars threading their way between the guard rails which line the entire track, it is impossible to avoid the thought that Monaco is no longer a suitable venue for a Formula 1 car to perform. Or maybe it is the other way round. Launching 800 horsepower projectiles around a track which is only nine metres wide seems senseless and the fact there has not been a serious accident for many years is a near miracle. A circuit like this would never be tolerated anywhere other than Monaco. Despite this, there has never been any talk of removing the star event from the calendar. The Monaco Grand Prix constitutes an anachronism, but everyone loves it, the drivers included and especially the sponsors. For the sport's cashiers it is the key to the vault of their season. They spare no expense to seduce their clients, whom they invite onto luxury yachts or the swanky balconies, which change hands for sacks of gold if they offer the best view of the action.

The organisers scratch their heads every year to come up with something new in their efforts to adapt the venue to the modern world of Formula 1. It is all in vain. Every year they resurface parts of the track, they subtly modify a kerb here or a corner there - for example the Swimming Pool "S" in 1997. But overall, there is little they can do with the raw materials at their disposal. *"Driving a Formula 1 car around Monaco is a bit like trying to fly a remote-control helicopter around your sitting room,"* joked Nelson Piquet. That was ten years ago, at the time when the turbo engines pushed out over 1000 horsepower during qualifying.

Time has made this circuit antiquated. But it is nothing new, as it was already thus back in the Fifties. In 1955, after Alberto Ascari's car plunged into the harbour, concerns were voiced that the circuit no longer met the required safety standards and those same voices reckoned we had witnessed the last Monaco Grand Prix.

"For us, it is no longer normal to race so close to the safety barriers," confirmed Michael Schumacher. *"It really is a terrible challenge to try and get the best out of the car. The slightest error does not cost you time, it costs you the race, because it automatically involves having an accident."*

On Thursday, Mika Hakkinen aired the same views. *"The most important thing here is to concentrate and stay calm, both on and off the track. Everyone wants a piece of us all through the weekend."*

In the past, only the best drivers have won on this treacherous track: in the last fifteen years, Ayrton Senna won six times, while Prost and Schumacher have four wins apiece. Proof of the natural selection process which can be seen at this track.

△
Mika Hakkinen was a victim of fate during qualifying for the Monaco Grand Prix. He systematically encountered traffic on his quick laps, effectively preventing him from joining the battle for pole position. However, one should point out that the track was deserted for almost half an hour after the lights went green. Why did the drivers not use up at least one of their four runs during this time?

«Let's get back to work» Jacques Villeneuve will quality 17th.
▽◁

"A little smile for the Formula 1 Yearbook? No problem!" The Mrs. Corinna Schumacher and Noriko Salo were as charming as ever on the harbour front in Monaco.
▽

Monaco by numbers

- Circuit length: 3.367 km
- 700 tonnes of grandstands
- 26 marshals posts around the track
- 590 track marshals, 220 firemen
- on the track: 100 doctors, 80 first-aiders, 40 ambulances, 40 nurses
- for spectators: 10 doctors, 20 nurses, 175 first-aiders
- 500 fire extinguishers, one every nine metres around the track
- 5530 tyres in the barriers
- 8 cranes
- 32 kilometres of guard rail
- 14,000 sq. metres of fencing

STARTING GRID

		M. SCHUMACHER 1'19"475
Jarno TRULLI 1'19"746	-1-	
		David COULTHARD 1'19"888
Heinz-H. FRENTZEN 1'19"961	-2-	
		Mika HÄKKINEN 1'20"241
R. BARRICHELLO 1'20"416	-3-	
		Jean ALESI 1'20"494
G. FISICHELLA 1'20"703	-4-	
		Ralf SCHUMACHER 1'20"742
Eddie IRVINE 1'20"743	-5-	
		Johnny HERBERT 1'20"792
Alexander WURZ 1'0"871	-6-	
		Mika SALO 1'21"561
Jenson BUTTON 1'21"605	-7-	
		Jos VERSTAPPEN 1'21"738
Pedro de la ROSA 1'21"832	-8-	
		Jacques VILLENEUVE 1'21"848
Nick HEIDFELD 1'22"017	-9-	
		Pedro DINIZ 1'22"136
Ricardo ZONTA 1'22"324	-10-	
		Marc GENÉ 1'23"721
Gaston MAZZACANE 1'23"794	-11-	

Five out of five for driving

And that made five! After victories in Australia, Brazil, San Marino and Nurburgring, Michael Schumacher continued his winning ways in Montreal with a fifth visit to the top of the podium.

It was some compensation for the disappointment of Monaco, where he was forced to retire while leading.

It has to be said, his Ferrari did not appear to be too reliable in Montreal. It managed to hold out to the end of Sunday afternoon, but only just, which was cause for concern for the Reds. Meanwhile, McLaren was unable to profit from the situation. They would have to wait a bit longer...

GRAND PRIX AIR CANADA
MONTRÉAL

David, the master of Magny Cours

David Coulthard and Michael Schumacher have a polite loathing for one another. Every single one of their attempts at reconciliation usually only lasts until the following grand prix. In Magny Cours, on Saturday after qualifying, the two men were deep in conversation; a rare sight indeed, given they hardly ever speak. By Sunday, this tender moment was nothing but a distant memory by the time the red lights went out. Moving across Coulthard's bows, Schumacher forced the Scotsman to lift off to avoid a collision. A few laps later, the Ferrari squeezed the McLaren to the outside of the hairpin. David was not amused, waving a fist and even a finger at Michael.

The little war between the two men had just kicked off again. It was Mika Hakkinen, an interested observer, who might turn the situation to his own advantage in the future. In the meantime, it was David Coulthard who took advantage of the Ferrari's problems to take his third grand prix win of the season.

MOBIL 1 GRAND PRIX DE FRANCE
MAGNY-COURS

The Scuderia in efficient mode during the qualifying session. The mechanics' ballet during a grand prix is perfectly choreographed, even when both cars come into the pits at the same time.

A good atmosphere in Magny Cours. Despite the broiling sun and heat, the crowd enjoyed the spectacle of qualifying.

Friday was Ralf Schumacher's 25th birthday. The Williams team had prepared a giant cake and brother Michael was keen to join the festivities. But the atmosphere was suspicious as Ralf was convinced his brother was planning the cake-in-face scenario. He was not wrong and the chocolate was flying

Michael Schumacher on pole

A nice trio!

"I don't really like this circuit. It's not too bad, but when it's hot, it's a pain." Michael Schumacher did not have much to say after Saturday's qualifying.

It had all gone well for him and he was quickest, end of story. *"I am very happy with the way the day went. We did a lot of work here in testing. We were ready and simply fine-tuned our settings. You have to be careful not to rely too much on what you have done here before, because the track is constantly changing."*

Actually, the German was never put under any pressure. He set his time in the first half hour and was never caught. The track got slower because of the intense heat that affected the Nevers track. At the last moment, David Coulthard got somewhere near his time, but was unable to improve on it. *"I don't think I could have gone any quicker if I had to,"* confessed Schumacher. *"We did not change much on the car, but we fully understand its handling now. We don't have any specific worries for tomorrow. Of course it will be a long tough race, but it should be alright."*

In second place, Coulthard could not say the same. Since the start of Friday's practice, the MP4/15 faced a number of problems. On Saturday morning, his mechanics had to change his engine, before discovering a fuel pump failure, which meant he had to qualify in the spare

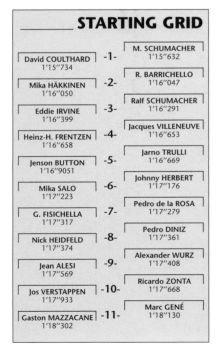

car. *"It was set up for Mika and it was not easy to adapt it to suit me,"* complained the Scotsman. *"But I think the race should go well for us."* In third place, Rubens Barrichello was very pleased to be starting from the second row. *"I think Magny Cours is a lucky circuit for me,"* opined the Brazilian. *"Last year I was on pole position and this year, I am third. It's all going well."*

Over at Prost Grand Prix, on the other hand, everything was going badly. Jean Alesi had only managed to qualify 18th for his home grand prix and he was not in his usual good humour. His throttle pedal jammed open which did not make his job any easier. The Peugeot engineers were facing an all-nighter to try and find the cause of the trouble.

Mika Hakkinen struggles

The two silver arrows were not far behind, but once again they had been beaten by the Ferraris on the grid of the French Grand Prix. For the fourth time in a row, David Coulthard did a better job than his team-mate. Mika Hakkinen was fourth, trailing Rubens Barrichello by the infinitesimal margin of three ridiculous thousandths of a second.

Nevertheless, the Finn had not been in the top three on the grid since the European Grand Prix.

Once again on Saturday, he attributed this poor performance to minor set up problems.

"In one way, it was a very disappointing session for me," he offered. *"But in another way, it was better today than yesterday when I was only 14thfastest. Now, I will have to sit down with my engineers to try and solve my problems. At the moment, the car's settings do not suit me at all."*

The Finn evidently felt the season was slipping away from him, because the day after this race, he headed off to the McLaren factory in Woking to try and sort things out. This plan of action did the trick as we would see in Austria two weeks later.

STARTING GRID

David COULTHARD 1'15"734	-1-	M. SCHUMACHER 1'15"632	
Mika HÄKKINEN 1'16"050	-2-	R. BARRICHELLO 1'16"047	
Eddie IRVINE 1'16"399	-3-	Ralf SCHUMACHER 1'16"291	
Heinz-H. FRENTZEN 1'16"658	-4-	Jacques VILLENEUVE 1'16"653	
Jenson BUTTON 1'16"9051	-5-	Jarno TRULLI 1'16"669	
Mika SALO 1'17"223	-6-	Johnny HERBERT 1'17"176	
G. FISICHELLA 1'17"317	-7-	Pedro de la ROSA 1'17"279	
Nick HEIDFELD 1'17"374	-8-	Pedro DINIZ 1'17"361	
Jean ALESI 1'17"569	-9-	Alexander WURZ 1'17"408	
Jos VERSTAPPEN 1'17"933	-10-	Ricardo ZONTA 1'17"668	
Gaston MAZZACANE 1'18"302	-11-	Marc GENÉ 1'18"130	

A one-two for McLaren and a third win this season for David Coulthard.

The silver arrows' revenge

The championship looked to be in the bag already for Michael Schumacher. A 22 point lead in the Drivers' Championship, pole position for the French Grand Prix, confidence at bursting point; nothing seemed likely to stop the victorious march to glory for Ferrari number 3 at Magny Cours. The German had virtually said as much: if the weather did not do anything unexpected, then he was confident as to his chances of winning.

Indeed, all went well at the start. The Scuderia led the dance for the first twenty laps with Schumacher ahead of Rubens Barrichello. David Coulthard, who had qualified on the front row was tailing them. *"I made a good start but Michael moved over on me and I had to lift off. It's not a very sporting attitude, but what could I do?"* On lap 22, the McLaren man managed to sneak by Barrichello under braking for the Adelaide hairpin.

Catching Schumacher, he made his first attempt at a passing move on lap 34.

Hogging the inside line, the Ferrari then squeezed the McLaren to the outside of the hairpin. Thanks to the on-board camera it was evident that Coulthard was not very impressed with this move, waving his fist at his rival before "giving him the finger." *"I must apologise for letting everyone see how angry I was,"* he regretted in the post-race conference. *"It was not a very nice gesture to make, especially as I know a lot of children watch the grands prix. But I was expecting to hold the outside line and I did not expect to be pushed aside by Michael. I was furious with him."*

Six laps later, this time going down the inside, the move paid off, although the two cars did actually touch. *"There's nothing to say really, it was a clean fight,"* added Coulthard. From then on, the road to victory lay ahead of him and he

was never worried all the way to the chequered flag. His lead was so comfortable at this point that the team gave him the "easy" board, indicating he should back off a bit.

Mika Hakkinen was happy to be second. *"I've got no complaints. We had the quickest car on the track."* The Finn was thus hinting that he could have passed Michael Schumacher in the closing stages of the race. *"I was watching his lines to decide the best place to pass him. Then, when he retired, I thought about trying to catch David. But, I told myself we were first and second and we had it in the bag, so it was silly to risk everything when I needed those six points."*

Thanks to this win, Coulthard was now within just twelve points of Michael Schumacher, with eight races still to go. The end of the season looked like being rather more exciting than it had seemed two hours earlier.

△
Third win of the year for David Coulthard, to go with victory at Silverstone and Monaco. The eternal Number Two is beginning to dream of world championships.

Grey faces in the Red camp

Exhausted, worn out, call it what you will, Rubens Barrichello looked drained from the effort he had put in to the race at Magny Cours as he stepped out of his F1-2000. *"We were not expecting a race like this,"* puffed the Brazilian. *"This morning, after the warm-up, we thought everything was looking good. But, as it turned out, the McLarens proved to be clearly quicker in the heat this afternoon. It seems, the tyres held up better on their cars than on ours."*

Tyres were not the only culprits. By a strange turnaround, the two McLarens seemed to be far

more competitive and evolved a lot more over the French Grand Prix weekend than the Ferraris. After starting in the lead, Michael Schumacher had to give best to David Coulthard (see above.) All the same, he could have finished second if his engine had not let go on lap 59, when it dumped its oil over the rear tyres, which allowed Mika Hakkinen to get past as well. *"At the start of the race, I could control the situation, but then my tyres seemed to go off quicker than those of our rivals,"* he complained. *"In the end the engine failed. We will have to take a close*

look at everything that happened here, but it won't change anything for this race. That's racing." With Schumacher eliminated, Rubens Barrichello was now the only defender of the Scuderia's colours. *"Right at the start, I thought I could fight off Coulthard. But he was much quicker in a straight line and there was nothing I could do about him. And after Michael's problem, the team told me to slow my pace down, so as not to risk another failure."* Rubens also faced another problem, when he made his second pit-stop, which cost him around ten seconds. *"If it hadn't been for that, I think I could have finished ahead of Mika,"* he concluded.

For the Scuderia, it had been a catastrophic race, salvaged only in part by a third place. *"Of course, it's been a black weekend for us,"* was Sporting Director Jean Todt's summing up of the event. *"The unwritten rule of this 2000 championship is that, if we don't win, "they" do. It's always the same story. Right from the start of the season, we knew it would be tough all the way to the end and today's race provides proof of that."*

◁
Now you see what happens when the two Ferraris and the two McLarens race in a tight group. We understand there are 39 laps remaining (they all agree on that) and that Michael Schumacher has a 0.6 second lead over David Coulthard, who has an identical lead over Mika Hakkinen.

 **MOBIL 1 GRAND PRIX DE FRANCE**

Jenson Button does his stuff in Magny Cours. The very young Englishman never ceased to amaze in his first season of Formula 1. While many pundits reckon that experience is everything in this sport, Button proved that talent does not wait and that experience is no substitute for bottle.

He finished eighth in Magny Cours. The next two races would be even better, as Jenson went on to finish fifth in Austria and fourth in Germany.

MOBIL 1 GRAND PRIX DE FRANCE

Return to form

After Michael Schumacher's win in the Canadian Grand Prix a month earlier, it had all seemed so clear: with a 22 point lead over David Coulthard, a 24 point advantage over Mika Hakkinen, the mid-season point safely reached, and perfect form forecast for the foreseeable future with a good car, it was getting difficult to see what could possibly stop the German from galloping to his third world title.

The night after the Austrian Grand Prix, two races later, the situation had been reversed. On the Zeltweg toboggan run, the two McLaren-Mercedes had been untouchable, both in qualifying and in the race. The gulf they had pulled out over the Ferraris was more than enough to cause concern among the tifosi.

For Mika Hakkinen it was above all a relief. After a long time at less than full strength in personal performance terms, the Finn was back on song in Austria. He managed to out-qualify his team-mate for the first time in five grands prix and went on to win his first grand prix since Spain. It was a real return to form.

GROSSER A1 PREIS VON ÖSTERREICH
SPIELBERG

Bravo Rubinho

It was an improbable scenario. Rubens Barrichello had qualified way down in eighteenth spot. Evidently, Hockenheim would not be the scene of the Brazilian's first grand prix victory.
And yet it would! Thanks to a crazy race, a downpour, a lunatic crossing the track and a few mistakes from McLaren, "Rubinho" eventually emerged victorious on the Hockenheim Autobahn.
The podium ceremony was an incredibly emotional affair. Not only was it Barrichello's first win, it was also the first time the Brazilian national anthem had been played at a grand prix since the death of a certain Ayrton Senna, way back in 1994.

ROSSER MOBIL 1 PREIS VON DEUTSCHLAND
HOCKENHEIM

 **GROSSER MOBIL 1 PREIS VON DEUTSCHLAND**

Heinz-Harald Frentzen in the steaming sunny Hockenheim forest. The German had a catastrophic qualifying for his home grand prix, what with traffic and having his best time disallowed, after he had short-cut the chicane on a slower lap. In the race, he proved he could still do it, climbing as high as sixth by lap 39. The podium was in sight, when he was forced to retire with electrical problems. Maybe another time.

GROSSER MOBIL 1 PREIS VON DEUTSCHLAND

The Belgian Grand Prix did not start too well for Rubens Barrichello. Only tenth on the grid, the Brazilian was stuck behind Jacques Villeneuve for a long time. In the end, he managed to climb up as high as fourth thanks to an early pit stop. But in the end, a fuel pressure problem forced his retirement as he came in to refuel. Or had he run out of petrol?

FOSTER'S BELGIAN GRAND PRIX

The counter attack

After the crushing domination of the McLarens in Hungary and Belgium, Scuderia Ferrari managed to turn the situation around in Monza. Here, on the outskirts of Milan, Michael Schumacher's car was clearly a notch above the rest, with the McLarens giving away two or three tenths per lap.
In Monza, the Ferraris proved they were still in the running and that the championship was not a foregone conclusion for Mika Hakkinen. This came as such a relief to Michael Schumacher that, shortly after the race, he burst into tears in front of the world's media. It was further proof of the tension that reigned as the season drew to a close.

GRAN PREMIO CAMPARI D'ITALIA
MONZA

Having qualified on the front row five times from the Canadian to the Hungarian Grands Prix, David Coulthard ran into bother in Monza and could do no better than fifth.
In the race, any chance of winning the world championship evaporated when he was knocked out in the carnage at the second chicane. He will have to try again.

GRAN PREMIO CAMPARI D'ITALIA

INDIANAPOLIS

Having qualified on the front row five times from the Canadian to the Hungarian Grands Prix, David Coulthard ran into bother in Monza and could do no better than fifth.
In the race, any chance of winning the world championship evaporated when he was knocked out in the carnage at the second chicane. He will have to try again.

GRAN PREMIO CAMPARI D'ITALIA

Michael Schumacher in tears after the race.

Strong emotions in Monza

The Italian Grand Prix provided several emotional moments. To start with, there was the terrible crash on the first lap and to round off the day there was the sight of Michael Schumacher bursting into floods of tears in the post-race press conference.

At the start, while everyone had been worried about a first corner accident and all the photographers were there, lenses poised, the drama actually unfolded a few hundred metres further down the track.

In the braking area for the Campari chicane, the second corner on the track, Heinz-Harald Frentzen crashed heavily into the back of Rubens Barrichello's Ferrari. *"I was trying to pass Rubens, but he changed line and braked unexpectedly early,"* was the German's justification for the incident. *"There was no way I could avoid him and I feel very lucky to have got away with just a bruised knee."*

With his car sideways across the track, it collected his Jordan team-mate Jarno Trulli, who hit David Coulthard's McLaren. Finally, Pedro De La Rosa's Arrows came through the dust cloud to ram Johnny Herbert's Jaguar and barrel roll several times before landing in the gravel. In total, six cars were eliminated. None of the drivers was badly hurt, but a flying wheel cost the life of a fire marshal (see below.)

The race was instantly put on hold with arrival of the Safety Car, while the marshals set about clearing away the wrecks involved in the accident and also to allow the injured fireman to be moved.

Once underway again, the race became nothing more than a procession. Michael Schumacher gradually pulled away from Mika Hakkinen. This was a big surprise for everyone, including the German. After the podium ceremony, the enormity of what he had done seemed to sink in. In the post-race television unilateral conference, he was asked if the fact he had equalled Ayrton Senna's number of wins meant anything to him. Michael promptly started sobbing uncontrollably and even Mika appeared too moved to answer any questions.

It was only later that the German was able to explain this untypical outburst of emotion, saying it was due to the particular circumstances of this win. *"I think everyone can understand why I broke down. We are in Italy, in front of a crowd which gave me incredible support throughout the race. And we are back on track after being off the pace for several weeks. I cannot find the right words to express my feelings, but to be back on top, to be back in the fight for the championship is such a relief."*

Solid as a rock, Schumacher had never before shown his emotions in public. The fact he finally did it in front of TV cameras in Monza, illustrated the feeling of tension within the Ferrari camp. It also proved that the man regarded as a driving machine also had a human side. He emerged all the greater for it.

△
Michael Schumacher back on the podium. Talk about relieved.

▷
Six cars were knocked out in the second corner shunt. Here, seen from a helicopter, we see Frentzen's Jordan, Barrichello's Ferrari, De La Rosa's Arrows and Coulthard's McLaren.

Jos Verstappen and Alexander Wurz profited from the mayhem at the front of the field. The Dutchman played his cards right to move up to fourth place.
▽

△ *A wheel flies back onto the side of the track.*

The tragic death of a fire marshal

The carnage that broke out on the first lap of the Italian Grand Prix cost the life of a fire marshal who was there to watch over the safety of the drivers. Paulo Gislimberti, in his thirties died from fatal injuries received when he was hit by a wheel which flew off a Jordan. Hit on the head and in the chest, he was transported to Monza hospital where he died in the emergency room that afternoon.

On Sunday evening, the Italian police impounded all the cars involved in the accident, as they were considered as evidence in the enquiry which followed the tragic incident. With both its cars held in Monza, the Jordan team had to cancel a test session it was due to take part in at the Mugello circuit the following week.

Sauber miss out on the points again

The first lap accident could have provided the perfect opportunity for the Sauber team to score some points. Unfortunately, car problems prevented the Swiss outfit from profiting from the situation. Hit by Eddie Irvine at the first corner, Mika Salo suffered a left rear puncture. Having pitted for repairs, he felt his car was oversteering and he stopped again, having lost his engine cover.

The team fitted a new one and the Finn went back out onto the track. At the half distance, he again lost the engine cover and his car started to oversteer again, He finished seventh.

In the other C19, Pedro Diniz was also hit at the first corner. With a damaged nose on his Sauber, he had to fight all race long with a car that was twitchy under braking and slower down the straights. He finished eighth. Another missed opportunity.

PRACTICE TIMES

No	Drivers	Car/Engine/Chassis	Practice Friday	Pos.	Practice Saturday	Pos.	Qualifying	Pos.	Warm-up	Pos.
1.	Mika Häkkinen	McLaren/Mercedes/MP4-15/04	1'25"553	4°	1'24"142	2°	1'23"967	3°	1'26"513	2°
2.	David Coulthard	McLaren/Mercedes/MP4-15/05	1'25"796	5°	1'24"292	4°	1'24"290	5°	1'26"611	4°
3.	Michael Schumacher	Ferrari/F1-2000/205	1'25"117	2°	1'23"904	1°	1'23"770	1°	1'26"593	3°
4.	Rubens Barrichello	Ferrari/F1-2000/202	1'25"057	1°	1'24"199	3°	1'23"797	2°	1'27"233	7°
5.	Heinz-Harald Frentzen	Jordan/Mugen Honda/EJ10/5	1'26"763	14°	1'26"272	19°	1'24"786	8°	1'27"538	12°
6.	Jarno Trulli	Jordan/Mugen Honda/EJ10/6	1'25"390	3°	1'25"198	12°	1'24"477	6°	1'27"919	17°
7.	Eddie Irvine	Jaguar/R1/05	1'25"907	6°	1'25"064	10°	1'25"251	14°	1'27"711	14°
8.	Johnny Herbert	Jaguar/R1/06	1'26"634	12°	1'25"473	16°	1'25"388	18°	1'27"775	15°
9.	Ralf Schumacher	Williams/BMW/FW22/02	1'27"852	21°	1'24"352	5°	1'24"516	7°	1'27"984	18°
10.	Jenson Button	Williams/BMW/FW22/04	1'26"452	11°	1'24"515	6°	1'24"907	12°	1'27"339	9°
11.	Giancarlo Fisochella	Benetton/Playlife/B200/05	1'26"809	15°	1'24"644	7°	1'24"789	9°	1'27"833	16°
12.	Alexander Wurz	Benetton/Playlife/B200/03	1'27"093	18°	8'45"695	22°	1'25"150	13°	1'27"692	13°
14.	Jean Alesi	Prost/Peugeot/AP03/01	1'27"904	22°	1'25"299	13°	1'25"558	19°	1'28"198	19°
15.	Nick Heidfeld	Prost/Peugeot/AP03/02	1'27"135	19°	1'25"431	15°	1'25"625	20°	1'28"388	20°
16.	Pedro Diniz	Sauber/Petronas/C19/07	1'25"981	8°	1'25"407	14°	1'25"324	16°	1'27"398	10°
17.	Mika Salo	Sauber/Petronas/C19/05	1'26"293	10°	1'25"179	11°	1'25"322	15°	1'27"097	6°
18.	Pedro de la Rosa	Arrows/Supertec/A21/04	1'25"912	7°	1'25"508	17°	1'24"814	10°	1'27"457	11°
19.	Jos Verstappen	Arrows/Supertec/A21/05	1'26"020	9°	1'25"776	18°	1'24"820	11°	1'26"718	5°
20.	Marc Gené	Minardi/Fondmetal/M02/03	1'26"638	13°	1'26"295	20°	1'26"336	21°	1'28"534	21°
21.	Gaston Mazzacane	Minardi/Fondmetal/M02/04	1'27"468	20°	1'27"234	21°	1'27"360	22°	1'29"501	22°
22.	Jacques Villeneuve	BAR/Honda/002/04	1'26"906	16°	1'24"780	9°	1'24"238	4°	1'27"321	8°
23.	Ricardo Zonta	BAR/Honda/002/05	1'27"070	17°	1'24"672	8°	1'25"337	17°	1'26"448	1°

MAXIMUM SPEEDS

No	Drivers	P1 Qualifs	Pos	P1 Race	Pos	P2 Qualifs	Pos	P2 Race	Pos	Finish Qualifs	Pos	Finish Race	Pos	Trap Qualifs	Pos	Trap Race	Pos
1.	M. Häkkinen	336,80	7°	340,00	1°	340,20	8°	341,60	2°	325,3[illegible]	3°	323,60	3°	351,40	5°	355,00	3°
2.	D. Coulthard	336,20	9°	331,20	14°	338,80	11°	-	-	325,3[illegible]	4°	-	-	352,20	3°	286,70	16°
3.	M. Schum.	337,90	4°	336,10	7°	341,70	3°	338,90	6°	327,90	1°	324,20	2°	349,00	9°	353,10	7°
4.	R. Barrichello	340,50	1°	335,20	8°	342,30	2°	-	-	326,90	2°	-	-	352,80	1°	281,50	19°
5.	H.-H. Frentzen	329,10	22°	332,50	11°	335,70	19°	-	-	319,90	18°	-	-	315,00	17°	280,40	20°
6.	J. Trulli	332,70	16°	331,10	15°	338,60	12°	-	-	321,80	12°	-	-	343,50	20°	283,60	18°
7.	E. Irvine	332,10	19°	-	-	335,80	18°	-	-	318,80	20°	-	-	342,80	22°	268,50	21°
8.	J. Herbert	333,40	15°	317,50	21°	336,20	17°	57,30	16°	319,10	19°	-	-	343,50	21°	298,80	15°
9.	R. Schum.	333,50	14°	330,10	16°	336,60	15°	330,80	13°	321,40	13°	314,50	12°	346,00	13°	342,70	14°
10.	J. Button	335,00	11°	326,70	20°	339,30	10°	287,40	15°	324,20	5°	233,50	15°	347,60	10°	286,30	17°
11.	G. Fisichella	337,30	5°	330,00	17°	341,20	6°	334,20	9°	323,60	7°	316,70	8°	350,50	6°	348,30	9°
12.	A. Wurz	335,80	10°	333,70	10°	341,10	7°	332,70	12°	322,00	11°	316,40	9°	349,90	7°	349,90	8°
14.	J. Alesi	334,00	12°	337,60	5°	338,20	13°	340,00	4°	320,80	15°	320,10	7°	345,60	16°	354,20	6°
15.	N. Heidfeld	333,60	13°	331,30	13°	336,70	14°	333,90	10°	320,60	16°	313,70	13°	346,00	14°	348,10	10°
16.	P. Diniz	332,00	20°	337,70	4°	333,90	21°	339,80	5°	320,00	17°	320,20	6°	343,60	19°	354,30	5°
17.	M. Salo	332,30	18°	336,60	6°	336,30	16°	337,10	7°	320,90	14°	321,30	5°	346,20	11°	354,50	4°
18.	P. de la Rosa	337,00	6°	334,10	9°	341.30	4°	-	-	323,10	9°	-	-	351,60	4°	262,50	22°
19.	J. Verstappen	338,50	2°	338,00	3°	342.80	1°	341,90	1°	322,50	10°	321,60	4°	349,80	8°	357,30	1°
20.	M. Gené	332,50	17°	329,00	19°	334.00	20°	329,80	14°	318,20	21°	313,10	14°	345,90	15°	342,90	13°
21.	G. Mazzacane	331,40	21°	329,80	18°	333,60	22°	333,40	11°	317,60	22°	315,10	11°	344,10	18°	347,00	12°
22.	J. Villeneuve	336,80	8°	332,40	12°	341,20	5°	334,50	8°	323,50	8°	315,60	10°	346,10	12°	347,30	11°
23.	A. Zonta	338,30	3°	339,30	2°	340,10	9°	340,90	3°	324,00	6°	324,80	1°	352,30	2°	355,30	2°

CLASSIFICATION & RETIREMENTS

Pos	Drivers	Team	Time
1.	M. Schum.	Ferrari	1:27:31.638
2.	Häkkinen	McLaren Mercedes	+ 3.810
3.	R. Schum.	Williams BMW	+ 52.432
4.	Verstappen	Arrows	+ 59.938
5.	Wurz	Benetton Playlife	+ 67.426
6.	Zonta	BAR Honda	+ 69.296
7.	Salo	Sauber Petronas	+ 1 lap
8.	Diniz	Sauber Petronas	+ 1 lap
9.	Gené	Minardi Fondmetal	+ 1 lap
10.	Mazzacane	Minardi Fondmetal	+ 1 lap
11.	Fisichella	Benetton Playlife	+ 1 lap
12.	Alesi	Prost Peugeaot	+ 2 laps

Lap	Drivers	Team	Reason
1	Irvine	Jaguar	accident > Salo
1	de la Rosa	Arrows	accident
1	Frentzen	Jordan Mugen Honda	accident
1	Trulli	Jordan Mugen Honda	accident
1	Coulthard	McLaren Mercedes	accident
1	Barrichello	Ferrari	accident
2	Herbert	Jaguar	accident
11	Button	Williams BMW	soff
15	Villeneuve	BAR Honda	electrics
16	Heidfeld	Prost Peugeot	spin

FASTEST LAPS

	Drivers	Time	Lap
1.	Häkkinen	1'25"595	50
2.	M. Schum.	1'25"663	36
3.	Zonta	1'26"433	22
4.	R. Schum.	1'26"636	49
5.	Fisichella	1'26"731	46
6.	Wurz	1'26"869	44
7.	Verstappen	1'27"033	31
8.	Diniz	1'27"215	44
9.	Salo	1'27"297	26
10.	Alesi	1'27"978	47
11.	Villeneuve	1'28"038	14
12.	Gené	1'28"131	31
13.	Mazzacane	1'28"299	49
14.	Heidfeld	1'29"580	14
15.	Button	2'27"131	8

All results : © 2000 Fédération Internationale de l'Automobile, 2, Ch. Blandonnet, 1215 Genève 15, Suisse

LAP CHART

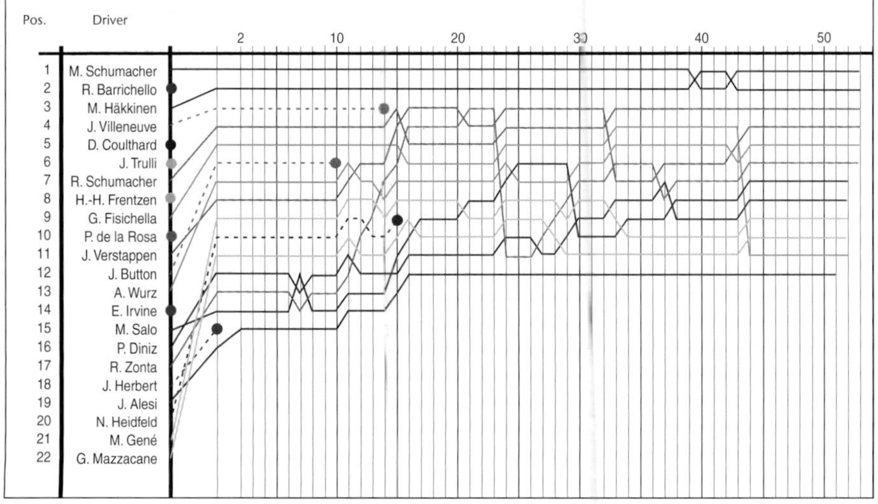
Pos.
Driver
2
10
20
30
40
50
M. Schumacher
R. Barrichello
M. Häkkinen
J. Villeneuve
D. Coulthard
J. Trulli
R. Schumacher
H.-H. Frentzen
G. Fisichella
P. de la Rosa
J. Verstappen
J. Button
A. Wurz
E. Irvine
M. Salo
P. Diniz
R. Zonta
J. Herbert
J. Alesi
N. Heidfeld
M. Gené
G. Mazzacane

PIT STOPS

	Drivers	Time	Lap	Stop n°
1.	Diniz	30"490	1	1
2.	Zonta	25"051	1	1
3.	Salo	48"537	1	1
4.	Salo	1'44"652	7	2
5.	Zonta	22"177	23	2
6.	Salo	26"217	29	3
7.	Mazzacane	26"364	29	1
8.	Alesi	23"469	29	1
9.	Verstappen	24"424	32	1
10.	Gené	22"811	33	1
11.	Zonta	21"549	36	3
12.	Diniz	26"309	37	2
13.	M. Schumacher	22"066	39	1
14.	Häkkinen	21"648	42	1
15.	Wurz	20"901	42	1
16.	R. Schumacher	21"140	43	1
17.	Fisichella	1'51"304	43	1

BRIDGESTONE

Quickest pit stop during the Italian Grand Prix, fitting four new Bridgestone tyres:

Alexander Wurz, Benetton, 20"901

THE CIRCUIT

FOURTEENTH ROUND

GRAN PREMIO CAMPARI D'ITALIA, MONZA

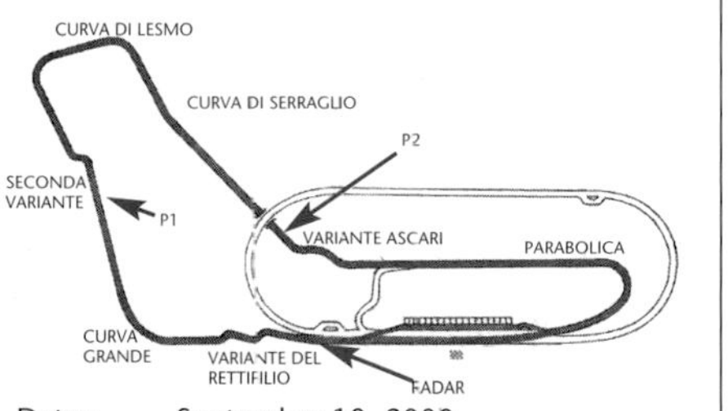
CURVA DI LESMO
CURVA DI SERRAGLIO
P2
SECONDA VARIANTE
P1
VARIANTE ASCARI
PARABOLICA
CURVA GRANDE
VARIANTE DEL RETTIFILIO
RADAR

Date : September 10, 2000
Length : 5793 meters
Distance : 53 laps, 306.764 km
Weather : sunny & hot, 26°

CHAMPIONSHIP

(after fourteen rounds)

Drivers :

1.	M. Häkkinen	80
2.	M. Schumacher	78
3.	D. Coulthard	61
4.	R. Barrichello	49
5.	R. Schumacher	24
6.	G. Fisichella	18
7.	J. Villeneuve	11
8.	J. Buton	10
9.	H.-H. Frentzen	7
10.	J. Trulli	6
	M. Salo	6
12.	J. Verstappen	5
13.	E. Irvine	3
14.	A. Wurz	2
	R. Zonta	2
	P. de la Rosa	2

Constructors :

1.	McLaren Mercedes	131
2.	Ferrari	127
3.	Williams BMW	34
4.	Benetton Playlife	20
5.	Jordan Mugen Honda	13
	BAR Honda	13
7.	Arrows	7
8.	Sauber Petronas	6
9.	Jaguar	3

RACE SUMMARY

- Starting from pole, Michael Schumacher keeps the lead. Behind him, Rubens Barrichello is overhauled by Mika Hakkinen.
- Just one kilometre into the race and a huge and dramatic accident knocks out six cars at the second chicane.
- The Safety Car then stays on track for 11 of the 53 laps.
- As the Safety Car pulls in, Jenson Button crashes out.
- The race is pretty dull from then on, but the tifosi massed around the track don't care. Schumacher gradually pulls out a gap which allows him to calmly refuel and win as he pleases.
- Second, Hakkinen was never able to challenge the German until the Ferrari man lifted off in the closing stages to make the gap look smaller than it really was.

WEEKEND GOSSIP

- **Williams for sale ?**

Was Frank Williams considering selling out to engine supplier BMW? While he had always denied this rumour up to now, Sir Frank seemed to have changed his mind. In the Sunday newspaper "The Observer," he declared that anything was possible. *"In life as in business, one should never say never,"* he concluded.

- **I'm here and I'm staying**

Mika Hakkinen denied rumours he would retire at the end of the season if he won a third consecutive title. *"I am still very motivated for 2001,"* he affirmed. A few weeks later in Malaysia, he seemed to admit that he had considered it, before denying it again. *"At first I did think I might stop, but finally I would have continued with or without the title,"* he said.

- **Monza on the wrist**

F1's official timekeeper, TAG-Heuer launched a replica of one of its watches from the Thirties, on Saturday and called it the "Monza." Ron Dennis and David Coulthard, whose McLaren team is sponsored by the Swiss company were each presented with one at a ceremony in the Monza Sporting Club on the outskirts of the Monza park.

- **Malaysian preview**

The Sauber team provided its Paddock Club area for the Malaysian GP organisers to host a press conference. The race was voted the best organised grand prix of the previous year and it was announced that the number of covered grandstand seats for this year had been increased from thirty two to seventy five thousand. This was so that spectators would not suffer from sunburn as they did in 1999.

- **Burti replaces Herbert**

Luciano Burti, Jaguar's Brazilian test driver was officially announced as the team's new driver for 2001, as a replacement for Johnny Herbert. The Englishman was considering switching to Indycars, but so far he had not found a new home.

- **Back to Paris?**

The FIA was considering quitting Geneva to return to Paris. The FIA had moved to Switzerland in 1999 partly to avoid French tax laws. With this problem apparently solved, it wanted to return to the Place de la Concorde in Paris and was looking for offices.

- **Flat out, flat out**

Monza confirmed its position as a temple of speed. On Saturday, Rubens Barrichello was quickest, clocked at 352.8 km/h just before the braking point for the first chicane. Bottom of the list was Eddie Irvine, credited with 342.8 km/h.

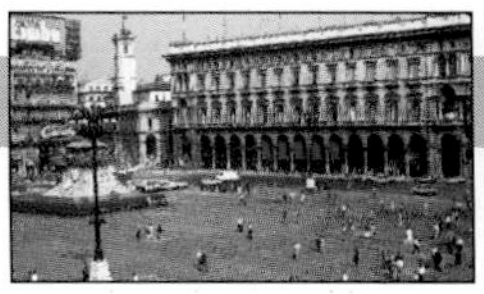

BACK IN THE USA

The big talking point of the weekend in America was quite simply that Formula 1 was back in America! It was almost ten years now since the grand prix cars had charged round the streets of Phoenix. The return was a total success. The grandstands of the incredible Indianapolis Motor Speedway were full to bursting point, with all the tickets having been sold in advance. A couple of hundred thousand American race fans were thus able to watch the wonder of a standing start. The whole weekend came with the added spice of a rancourous duel between Michael Schumacher and David Coulthard, which ended in victory for the German. With Mika Hakkinen forced to retire, the future was looking bright for Michael Schumacher.

THE SAP UNITED STATES GRAND PRIX
INDIANAPOLIS

> Michael Schumacher swooshes round the oval at Indianapolis. It might look impressive as a corner, but it provided few overtaking opportunities in the race.

Michael Schumacher out in front in qualifying.

In the slipstream

The Ferraris seemed ever so slightly more comfortable on the Indianapolis circuit than the McLarens, but the difference was so infinitesimal that the order could easily be reversed in the race.

During qualifying on Saturday, the two Ferrari drivers worked as a team to get Michael Schumacher on pole. Barrichello went round in front of his team leader, in order to tow him down the main straight, allowing the German to slipstream past. In the McLaren camp, it was Mika Hakkinen who helped David Coulthard, which knocked the Finn down a place, much to his satisfaction apparently. *"On this track it's better to start third, on the clean side of the circuit. Second place will start on the dirty side."*

The first corner was the subject of some concern among the drivers. *"It's a long way from the start to the first corner,"* argued Hakkinen. *"We will get there at high speed and I am worried that some drivers will miss their braking point. Everyone will want to be first through the first turn, especially as the*

track is very wide at that point."

At the pit lane entry however, the track was far from wide. *"It's scary. The track is bumpy and much too narrow,"* continued the Finn. *"If it rains, you could go off, end up on the grass and come back across the track."* To ease the problem, the organisers decided to move the start of the speed restricted zone further back.

Another unknown quantity would be the rain, which had threatened all through Saturday. *"Yes, the chance of rain worries me,"* admitted Schumacher. *"No one has ever raced in the wet here and there is a chance of streams running across the track."*

No greater chance of overtaking

The Indianapolis Motor Speedway represents the very essence of American motor racing. Built in 1909, the oval has run its famous 500 Mile race since 1911. In 1998, its owners embarked on a massive project of modernisation, including an infield circuit, a control tower and grandstands worthy of being called grand. *"We have invested 18*

million dollars in this work," indicated Tony George, the circuit owner. *"But it will take two years to complete."*

With its banked corner, the Indianapolis oval can lay claim to the longest straight of the season as the engines are at full throttle for 21 seconds.

One would think that would lead to some chance of overtaking during the race, especially as the track is wide enough at this point to accommodate several cars running alongside one another. Not to mention the fact that the banked turns theoretically allow for several different lines.

However, it seemed that these expectations were a touch optimistic. According to Michael Schumacher, there would be no more passing moves here than anywhere else. *"The corner leading onto the straight is too slow and we are not completely flat out in the long corner,"* he explained. *"The next straight is too short and the corner at the end is too wide to pass anyone under braking as there is no need to brake hard."*

STARTING GRID

R. BARRICHELLO 1'23"797	-1-	M. SCHUMACHER 1'23"770	
Jacques VILLENEUVE 1'24"238	-2-	Mika HÄKKINEN 1'23"967	
Jarno TRULLI 1'24"477	-3-	David COULTHARD 1'24"290	
Heinz-H. FRENTZEN 1'24"786	-4-	Ralf SCHUMACHER 1'24"516	
Pedro de la ROSA 1'24"814	-5-	G. FISICHELLA 1'24"789	
Jenson BUTTON 1'24"907	-6-	Jos VERSTAPPEN 1'24"820	
Eddie IRVINE 1'25"251	-7-	Alexander WURZ 1'25"150	
Pedro DINIZ 1'25"324	-8-	Mika SALO 1'25"322	
Johnny HERBERT 1'25"388	-9-	Ricardo ZONTA 1'25"337	
Nick HEIDFELD 1'25"625	-10-	Jean ALESI 1'25"558	
Gaston MAZZACANE 1'27"360	-11-	Marc GENÉ 1'261"336	

> Nick Heidfeld drives over a legend; the yard wide strip of bricks which runs across the track as a symbol of the circuit's old surface, which gave the oval its Brickyard nickname.

Michael Schumacher leads the race

And they're off! But it's a bad start for David Coulthard, who jumped the lights, requiring him to pit for a penalty a few laps later.

Thinking about something else...

With a one-two finish for Ferrari and Mika Hakkinen failing to finish, the Scuderia's sporting director Jean Todt could hardly have hoped for a more triumphant result.

It had not looked so easy at the start. Having anticipated the lights, Coulthard found himself in the lead. Knowing he would be called into the pits, he contented himself with delaying Schumacher so that Hakkinen could put the German under pressure. Eventually, the Ferrari man got bored with these tactics and muscled his way past going into the corner at the end of the straight.

With Coulthard out of the way and everyone having stopped for "slicks" the rain at the start having eased off, Schumacher found that Hakkinen was closing in fast. "We had set up the car to be quick down the straights and I don't think Mika could have passed me anyway," argued the German. Once his rival was out of the race, courtesy of an exploding Mercedes engine, no one really challenged the leader, his brother Ralf following some 12 seconds behind.

From then on, his race was a nice Sunday drive, interrupted by a major scare when he had a spec-

tacular spin with four laps to go. "I admit I wasn't concentrating. I was thinking about something else, but I better not say what," he laughed. "The team asked me to slow down as I had a 25 second lead over Rubens and I had not noticed the grass near the edge of the track. After that Ross suggested I concentrate and I told him I was wide awake now."

The German was looking good in the championship stakes, as the day delivered him an eight point lead with two races remaining.

A podium for HH

Jacques Villeneuve was almost on home turf in Indianapolis. Having won the Indianapolis 500 here in 1995, he was pretty much racing in front of the home crowd. In the race, he tried all he knew to get on the podium, but he missed out on it, beaten by half a second by Heinz-Harald Frentzen. For the German, this was a first podium (he was eventually classified 3rd in Brazil) in a difficult season. "It's a huge relief," he sighed after the race. "We have worked very hard this year, but we never made it, for different reasons every time."

All the same, it was a tough race for the German. "I never had two seconds to relax as I was always being attacked from behind." With seven laps to go, the Jordan was actually passed, but not for long, by Jacques Villeneuve. "Jacques was a bit too optimistic as he had no chance of getting by at this point."

David Coulthard - almost a bad boy

David Coulthard had a strange grand prix. He qualified on the front row, thanks to his team-mate towing him round the track, which meant the Scotsman started second, knowing he was on the dirty side of the track.

Furthermore, one week earlier, Ron Dennis had asked him to help his team-mate in the fight for the title. Could it be he had decided to deliberately jump the start to ensure he was ahead at the first corner? His explanations after the race were confusing enough to render this theory plausible. Shortly after the start, Coulthard certainly slowed dramatically, allowing Hakkinen to close on Schumacher. It was all classic team orders stuff. Michael Schumacher had done the very same thing in Malaysia a year earlier to help his team-mate Eddie Irvine.

But, when Schumacher tried to pass him at the end of the straight, Coulthard came close to being a very bad boy indeed. The German

had taken the tow and was coming down the outside. The McLaren man then moved over on the Ferrari, and appeared to try and push him off the track. His McLaren slid for a moment and almost ran into the Ferrari, which prompted the anger of the future world champion. "For David to slow me down in the slow section, I can understand. It's part of the game. But for him to run into me when I am running wide in the corner is really not correct."

There was no damage done to either car and DC managed to come up with a crazy excuse. "I think I was quicker than Michael, but my tyres were blistered, which is why he caught me so quickly", claimed the McLaren driver.

On the pit wall, Ron Dennis had been hoping that Coulthard's antics would allow Mika Hakkinen to take the lead. It didn't work out that way. But for a man who often complained about Ferrari's unsporting tactics, he would have to eat his words this time.

Michael Schumacher fights off the attentions of Mika Hakkinen. The German reckoned he could have held him off to the chequered flag, if the Finn had not retired.

Two red drivers, one yellow one and no greys. The Scuderia could not have been any happier about the colours on the podium.

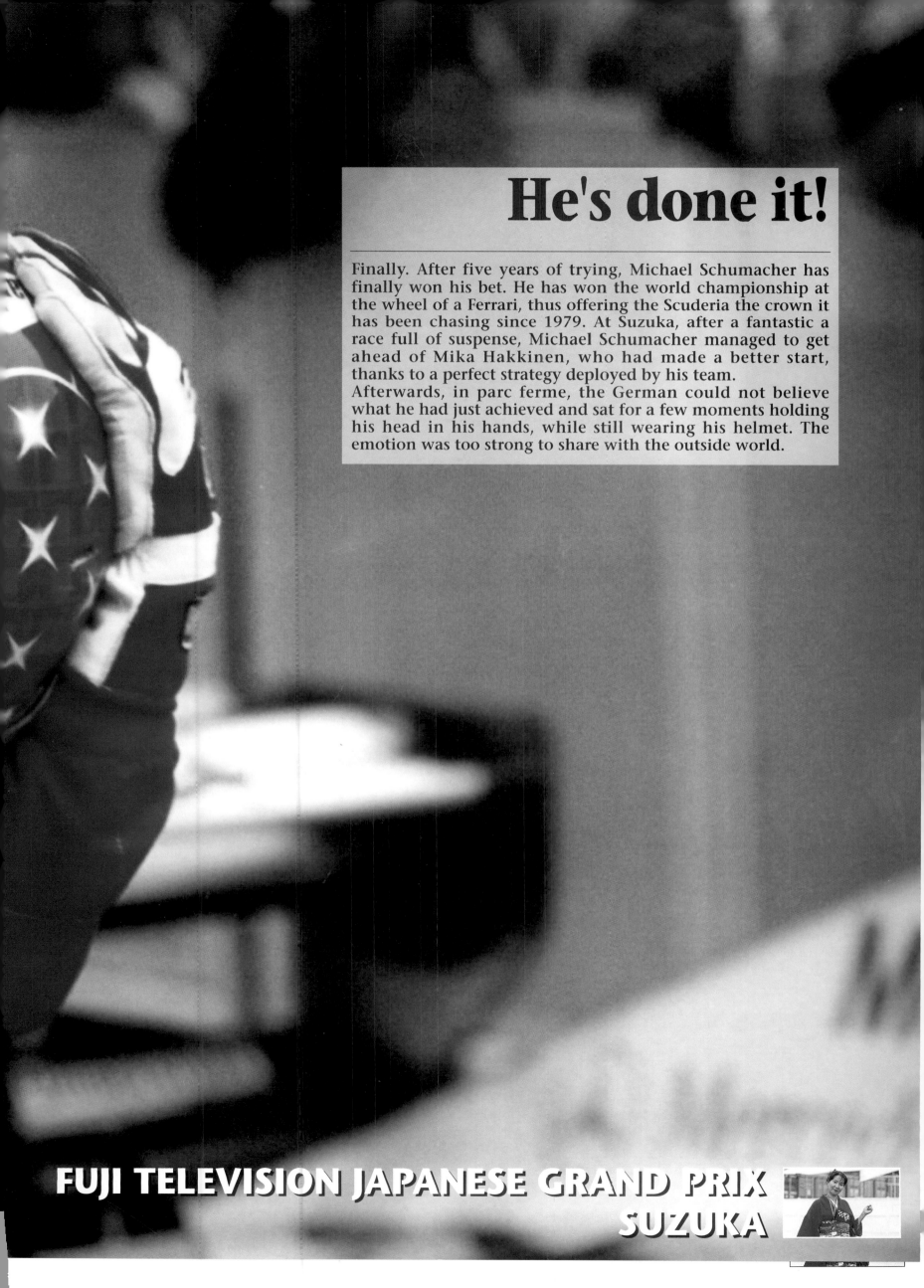

He's done it!

Finally. After five years of trying, Michael Schumacher has finally won his bet. He has won the world championship at the wheel of a Ferrari, thus offering the Scuderia the crown it has been chasing since 1979. At Suzuka, after a fantastic a race full of suspense, Michael Schumacher managed to get ahead of Mika Hakkinen, who had made a better start, thanks to a perfect strategy deployed by his team.

Afterwards, in parc ferme, the German could not believe what he had just achieved and sat for a few moments holding his head in his hands, while still wearing his helmet. The emotion was too strong to share with the outside world.

FUJI TELEVISION JAPANESE GRAND PRIX SUZUKA

FUJI TELEVISION JAPANESE GRAND PRIX

Scenes of happiness in Suzuka. For several hours after the end of the race, it was party time and smiles all round in the Ferrari camp. Here are some choice moments.

FUJI TELEVISION JAPANESE GRAND PRIX

Champions!

Having secured the Drivers' title in Suzuka, Scuderia Ferrari did the double in Kuala Lumpur by adding the Constructors' crown to their tally.

All the Italian team required was three little points. They did much better in fact, as Michael Schumacher was in a class of his own, taking his ninth win of the season. It was total party time for the Scuderia on Sunday night.

**PETRONAS MALAYSIAN GRAND PRIX
KUALA LUMPUR**

▷
Ninth pole position of the season for Michael Schumacher. And this time, the German managed to pull out a more than respectable advantage over Mika Hakkinen.

Third place in the championship was still up for grabs

Number nine for Michael

STARTING GRID

Mika HÄKKINEN 1'37"860	**-1-** M. SCHUMACHER 1'37"397
R. BARRICHELLO 1'37"896	**-2-** David COULTHARD 1'37"889
Jacques VILLENEUVE 1'38"653	**-3-** Alexander WURZ 1'38"644
Ralf SCHUMACHER 1'38"739	**-4-** Eddie IRVINE 1'38"696
Heinz-H. FRENTZEN 1'38"988	**-5-** Jarno TRULLI 1'38"909
Johnny HERBERT 1'39"331	**-6-** Ricardo ZONTA 1'39"158
Pedro de la ROSA 1'39"443	**-7-** G. FISICHELLA 1'39"387
Jenson BUTTON 1'39"563	**-8-** Jos VERSTAPPEN 1'39"489
Jean ALESI 1'40"065	**-9-** Mika SALO 1'39"591
Pedro DINIZ 1'40"521	**-10-** Nick HEIDFELD 1'40"148
Gaston MAZZACANE 1'42"078	**-11-** Marc GENÉ 1'40"662

In order to win the Constructors' Championship in Sepang, Scuderia Ferrari only needed to pick up three little points - something it had managed to do in every race since the start of the season.

2000 would not be David Coulthard's year, any more than it had been in 1999, 1998 or 1997. Every year since the Scotsman signed up with McLaren-Mercedes in 1996, he had always claimed to be aiming for nothing less than the world championship.

At the end of each season, having been outpaced by Mika Hakkinen, he would cite his comparative lack of experience in F1, when compared with the Finn. He currently has 106 grands prix starts under his belt, but this was still his excuse for not beating Mika.

In Sepang, as the final grand prix of the season approached, Coulthard would have to fight off Rubens Barrichello, to hang onto third place in the championship.

He apparently cared not a jot for this familiar third spot. *"This weekend, I will simply be aiming to finish the season on a high note,"* he said. *"I am not thinking about my final position in the championship. Because finishing third or fourth means nothing to me. It has absolutely no effect on my bank balance."*

The Scotsman had actually finished third on three previous occasions; in 1995, 1997 and 1998. *"I have come third before, so it means very little,"* he continued. *"I have never been runner-up or champion, which would represent real progress."*

Coulthard put part of the blame for this year's failure on his team's shoulders. As usual. *"I made a few mistakes, but the team also made mistakes, in terms of strategy, especially when it came to the decision regarding when to bring me in for my pit-stops. That's why I scored less points in the second half of the season."*

On the Sepang circuit, Rubens Barrichel-lo tried all he knew to steal third place off the Scotsman. But it looked like being a tall order. *"I have to win with David finishing out of the points,"* analysed the Brazilian. *"It will not be easy, but I will give it my best shot, especially as David does not seem to care about being third."*

When Saturday dawned, it was obvious that Michael Schumacher was in no mood to pussyfoot around, as he set a qualifying time almost half a second quicker than the McLarens. He did it easily, not even bothering to use up all the 12 laps available to him. *"Actually, it wasn't quite as easy as it looked,"* he explained. *"The reason I did so few laps is I didn't have time to go out for a final run. We started late in the session as the track was very dirty, so it would have been pointless going out any earlier. We didn't make any major changes to the car during the session. I tried changing the rear wing but I went back to the original. Anyway, the car seemed quite well balanced."*

the title is in the bag....before the start

Michael Schumacher had predicted it would be a piece of cake. So it turned out, as Ferrari had no problems securing its second consecutive Constructors' title in Sepang.

For McLaren to win, its drivers needed to finish first and second, with Ferrari scoring only two points. It smacked of mission impossible and it was aborted at the moment the red lights went out. Mika Hakkinen jumped the start and was given a ten second stop-go penalty, which he came in for five laps later. *"I knew the Constructors' Championship was lost from the start,"* confirmed David Coulthard after the race. *"When I saw Mika move forward at the red lights, I knew he would be penalised and that we would not do the double."*

Having got away better than anyone else, for obvious reasons, Hakkinen decided to let his team-mate and both Ferraris go by him on the first lap after the Safety Car had come in after a second lap accident. *"My car moved a bit when the red lights were on and there was nothing I could do,"* explained the Finn. *"It's a shame, because I think my one stop strategy was the right one. I think I would have won the race."*

Out in front, Coulthard led Schumacher by around five seconds. The Scot came in for a very early first stop and Ferrari re-ran their Suzuka strategy. It was equally successful this time. While Coulthard was back on track with a full tank, Schumacher stepped up the pace with a lighter car and low fuel.

When the German made his pit stop, he managed to emerge in the lead. From then on, all he had to do was keep a watchful eye on his mirrors, as Coulthard was never far behind. *"I was flat out from start to finish,"* recounted Michael. *"I didn't have a moment to catch my breath or slow down a fraction. David did not make life easy for me. But the main thing is we have won this championship. Everyone in the team has worked very hard to get it and they well deserve it."*

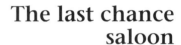

△
"We've won!" The entire Ferrari team clambered onto the pit wall to salute Michael Schumacher as he crossed the line.

The last chance saloon

◁
Both Ferrari drivers and Ross Brawn donned red wigs to brighten up the podium ceremony.

This race was the last chance for several teams to try and redeem themselves after a bad season. For the Prost outfit, it was the final opportunity to try and beat Minardi in the Constructors' Championship. All it would take was a seventh place. But even this was too much to ask for the aptly named Blues. Nick Heidfeld was involved in the second corner pile up and had to retire, while Jean Alesi was also caught up in the crash, but soldiered on to finish eleventh.

The final points of the season went to Jacques Villeneuve fifth and Eddie Irvine sixth. In his final grand prix, Johnny Herbert had a huge shunt in the other Jaguar. He emerged with a bruised knee. It could have been much worse. *"I had to be lifted into the car at the start of my career, so I suppose it was inevitable I would be carried out of the car at the end,"* joked the ever cheerful Englishman.

The last start of the season and another average one from Michael Schumacher, who was caught out by both McLarens.
▽

A festival of engine parts. These days it has become very difficult to photograph what goes on in a Formula 1 power plant, as the teams jealously guard their secrets, hiding them away under covers.

Alexander Wurz was announced as the replacement for France's Olivier Panis as the third driver in the McLaren team for 2001. "With Olivier, we felt the benefit of working with an experienced driver," commented McLaren managing director, Martin Whitmarsh. For his part, Wurz sounded enthusiastic about his new life. No sooner signed than dressed for the part. Late on Friday afternoon, he paraded in full team kit alongside Hakkinen and Coulthard.

David makes peace with Michael

The chequered flag falls, the drivers complete their slowing down lap and climb out of the cockpit in parc ferme. Having donned red wigs, the two Ferrari drivers head for the compulsory post-race weigh-in. It was in this relatively private area, only relatively, as the TV cameras picked it up, that David Coulthard had a little chat with Michael Schumacher. The two men had their arms round one another and both were smiling broadly. It was a strange sight, given their violent exchange of views throughout the season. *"I was apologising to Michael,"* explained Coulthard later. *"I congratulated him on his title and I apologised for what had gone on between us this year. I criticised him a lot through the media, when I had told myself I wouldn't act like that. But I suppose one gets lazier with age and I couldn't be bothered to go down to the Ferrari garage and talk to him face to face. It was embarrassing, so I complained to the press. But I realise he is a great champion and I might have been wrong with some of my remarks. In future, I will go and see him if I have any complaints. I wanted to do it in Japan, but our paths never crossed. I wanted to end this business on a positive note."*

Second place in the race, was good enough for David Coulthard to finish third in the 2000 Drivers' Championship.

Michael strips off

Tan Sri Dato Basir, the boss of Kuala Lumpur Airport had invited the entire Formula 1 paddock; mechanics, engineers, drivers and press, to celebrate the end of the season at a giant party held in the VIP boxes above the pits on Sunday night. He could not have guessed his invitation would lead to one of the most riotous end-of-season bashes.

All the Ferrari crew were there, wearing the obligatory red wigs, seen earlier on the podium. The big surprise came at around 8 o'clock, when the company president Luca di Montezemolo made an appearance. He had arrived that same day in Kuala Lumpur, but had remained tucked away in his hotel room, watching the race on the box, thinking his presence at the track might bring bad luck on the team. He had attended the final round in 1997, 1998 and 1999 and each time it ended in failure. Michael Schumacher was in wild mood and ripped the trousers of the Mercedes chief, the exuberant Norbert Haug. This led to all-out war, which left everyone with their trousers in shreds and bare flesh everywhere. The German driver had promised a wild night and he was true to his word. There were several major hangovers among those queuing at airline check-ins the next morning.

Humble pie on the McLaren menu

It had all begun at the Japanese Grand Prix, when Ron Dennis complained to the press about the appointment of Roberto Causo as one of the race stewards. The previous year, Causo had represented Ferrari in the Malaysian barge board affair and Dennis had doubts about his impartiality.

In Sepang, FIA President Max Mosley replied to Dennis' accusations by means of an open letter distributed in the media centre. It was a stinging reply, designed to put the McLaren boss back in his place. *"No one in the FIA objects to criticism, particularly if it is properly thought out and rational. But there comes a point when the interests of Formula One as a sport are threatened. You do a lot of damage when, as a team principal, you constantly suggest that the F1 world championship is not properly or fairly run. This discourages new sponsors and new fans."*
Further on, the letter claimed that attacks on Causo were absurd. *"Your complaint seems to be that he is Italian. He is just one of our stewards, but the race director, the observer the two software specialists, the fuel analyst, the chief medical officer (not to mention the FIA President and the*

Commercial Rights Holder) all share the same British nationality as you and your team. Do you not see the absurdity of your position? Imagine what would happen if Italy and Ferrari, not to mention Benetton, Jordan, Minardi, Prost and Sauber took the same line about the British as you do about the Italians. If we eliminate Italian stewards we must, if we are to be consistent, also eliminate not just British, Finnish and German stewards, but any other official who shares nationality with a team or team...This was really not one of your more inspired ideas."
Mosley's letter continued in similar vein attacking Dennis' criticism of the use of the black flag for drivers conducting themselves in an unsporting manner. It ended with the suggestion that the McLaren boss might like to set up his own alternative series!
The next day, Dennis wrote a letter in which he said he never intended damaging a sport to which he had dedicated his life. He also apologised to Roberto Causo for any hurt caused. What with Coulthard apologising to Schumacher after the race, it was a humble pie weekend for McLaren.

PRACTICE TIMES

No	Drivers	Car/Engine/Chassis	Practice Friday	Pos.	Practice Saturday	Pos.	Qualifying	Pos.	Warm-up	Pos.
1.	Mika Häkkinen	McLaren/Mercedes/MP4-15/06	1'40"262	1°	1'38"348	4°	1'37"860	2°	1'40"080	2°
2.	David Coulthard	McLaren/Mercedes/MP4-15/02	1'40"498	3°	1'38"109	1°	1'37"889	3°	1'40"393	4°
3.	Michael Schumacher	Ferrari/F1-2000/205	1'40"276	2°	1'38"203	2°	1'37"397	1°	1'40"246	3°
4.	Rubens Barrichello	Ferrari/F1-2000/200	1'40"877	4°	1'38"955	5°	1'37"896	4°	1'41"161	6°
5.	Heinz-Harald Frentzen	Jordan/Mugen Honda/EJ10/6	1'41"751	10°	1'40"551	20°	1'38"988	10°	1'42"282	19°
6.	Jarno Trulli	Jordan/Mugen Honda/EJ10/5	1'41"304	5°	1'39"382	10°	1'38"909	9°	1'41"888	13°
7.	Eddie Irvine	Jaguar/R1/05	1'42"141	14°	1'39"110	7°	1'38"696	7°	1'41"527	9°
8.	Johnny Herbert	Jaguar/R1/06	1'42"113	13°	1'39"107	6°	1'39"331	12°	1'41"332	8°
9.	Ralf Schumacher	Williams/BMW/FW22/06	1'41"493	6°	1'39"430	11°	1'38"739	8°	1'42"372	20°
10.	Jenson Button	Williams/BMW/FW22/04	1'42"012	12°	1'39"230	8°	1'39"563	16°	1'41"791	12°
11.	Giancarlo Fisichella	Benetton/Playlife/B200/06	1'41"593	8°	1'39"849	17°	1'39"387	13°	1'41"956	14°
12.	Alexander Wurz	Benetton/Playlife/B200/03	1'41"679	9°	1'38"318	3°	1'38"644	5°	1'40"916	5°
14.	Jean Alesi	Prost/Peugeot/AP03/01	1'42"868	18°	1'39"988	19°	1'40"065	18°	1'42"177	18°
15.	Nick Heidfeld	Prost/Peugeot/AP03/02	1'43"786	22°	1'39"794	13°	1'40"148	19°	1'42"731	21°
16.	Pedro Diniz	Sauber/Petronas/C19/07	1'42"457	16°	1'39"916	18°	1'40"521	20°	1'41"755	11°
17.	Mika Salo	Sauber/Petronas/C19/05	1'43"284	19°	1'39"839	16°	1'39"591	17°	1'41"559	10°
18.	Pedro de la Rosa	Arrows/Supertec/A21/02	1'42"254	15°	1'39"798	14°	1'39"443	14°	1'42"104	15°
19.	Jos Verstappen	Arrows/Supertec/A21/04	1'41"914	11°	1'39"812	15°	1'39"489	15°	1'42"155	17°
20.	Marc Gené	Minardi/Fondmetal/M02/03	1'43"655	21°	1'41"806	21°	1'40"662	21°	1'42"105	16°
21.	Gaston Mazzacane	Minardi/Fondmetal/M02/04	1'43"424	20°	1'42"370	22°	1'42"078	22°	1'43"621	22°
22.	Jacques Villeneuve	BAR/Honda/002/04	1'42"649	17°	1'39"337	9°	1'38"653	6°	1'4[illegible]"309	7°
23.	Ricardo Zonta	BAR/Honda/002/01	1'41"497	[illegible]°	1'39"440	12°	1'39"158	11°	1'40"032	1°

MAXIMUM SPEEDS

No	Drivers	P1 Qualifs	Pos	P1 Race	Pos	P2 Qualifs	Pos	P2 Race	Pos	Finish Qualifs	Pos	Finish Race	Pos	Trap Qualifs	Pos	Trap Race	Pos
1.	M. Häkkinen	292,30	2°	293,70	3°	141,00	18°	140,40	15°	263,40	14°	267,70	1°	296,30	9°	303,00	4°
2.	D. Coulthard	292,30	3°	294,90	2°	138,00	22°	138,10	17°	266,80	3°	266,10	3°	301,70	1°	305,50	1°
3.	M. Schum.	291,50	5°	290,00	13°	139,90	20°	141,80	9°	265,20	7°	262,30	12°	300,10	3°	297,60	16°
4.	R. Barrichello	290,70	7°	288,60	15°	141,60	15°	142,20	8°	264,70	10°	262,90	8°	298,40	5°	298,60	14°
5.	H.-H. Frentzen	287,50	13°	287,90	17°	140,30	19°	137,80	18°	265,00	8°	258,80	18°	295,40	10°	296,50	18°
6.	J. Trulli	288,40	10°	291,70	8°	142,40	12°	139,70	16°	265,60	6°	262,80	9°	297,60	8°	300,10	12°
7.	E. Irvine	286,90	15°	293,40	4°	146,10	3°	145,30	2°	263,00	16°	262,90	7°	293,70	17°	301,40	9°
8.	J. Herbert	288,90	8°	290,80	11°	143,20	9°	140,90	13°	264,50	11°	262,50	10°	298,00	7°	301,40	8°
9.	R. Schum.	290,90	6°	291,00	10°	144,50	6°	141,10	11°	266,50	4°	262,30	11°	298,30	6°	301,70	7°
10.	J. Button	287,60	12°	289,50	14°	142,50	11°	135,90	19°	264,90	9°	260,00	17°	294,50	12°	298,50	15°
11.	G. Fisichella	287,70	11°	286,30	19°	143,30	8°	144,20	4°	263,00	15°	258,80	19°	295,40	11°	297,10	17°
12.	A. Wurz	286,30	17°	291,50	9°	141,40	17°	144,00	5°	263,70	13°	263,90	6°	294,10	14°	300,60	10°
14.	J. Alesi	283,50	21°	290,00	12°	139,90	21°	140,50	14°	261,80	17°	261,50	14°	292,30	20°	302,80	5°
15.	N. Heidfeld	286,70	16°	-	-	143,00	10°	-	-	261,60	18°	-	-	293,20	19°	238,80	21°
16.	P. Diniz	283,60	20°	-	-	141,50	16°	-	-	258,50	22°	-	-	290,40	22°	236,50	22°
17.	M. Salo	285,10	19°	296,30	1°	146,00	4°	142,50	6°	261,60	19°	262,10	13°	292,20	21°	303,50	3°
18.	P. de la Rosa	293,10	1°	-	-	145,00	5°	-	-	267,70	2°	-	-	299,70	4°	239,90	20°
19.	J. Verstappen	291,70	4°	293,30	5°	148,00	1°	144,90	3	273,10	1°	265,40	5°	301,10	2°	304,70	2°
20.	M. Gené	287,10	14°	288,20	16°	146,90	2°	141,70	10°	261,50	20°	261,00	15°	294,50	13°	301,70	6°
21.	G. Mazzacane	281,90	22°	286,90	18°	142,10	14°	140,90	12°	259,90	21°	260,40	16°	293,30	18°	296,20	19°
22.	J. Villeneuve	288,40	9°	291,80	7°	142,30	13°	142,30	7°	265,80	5°	266,00	4°	293,70	15°	300,10	13°
23.	A. Zonta	286,00	18°	292,90	6°	144,00	7°	146,30	1°	264,30	12°	266,40	2°	293,70	16°	300,60	11°

CLASSIFICATION & RETIREMENTS

Pos	Drivers	Team	Time
1.	M. Schum.	Ferrari	1:35:54.235
2.	Coulthard	McLaren Mercedes	+0.732
3.	Barrichello	Ferrari	+ 18.879
4.	Häkkinen	McLaren Mercedes	+35.269
5.	Villeneuve	BAR Honda	+ 70.692
6.	Irvine	Jaguar	+ 72.568
7.	Wurz	Benetton Playlife	+89.314
8.	Salo	Sauber Petronas	+ 1 lap
9.	Fisichella	Benetton Playlife	+ 1 lap
10.	Verstappen	Arrows	+ 1 lap
11.	Alesi	Prost Peugeot	+ 1 lap
12.	Trulli	Jordan Mugen Honda	+ 1 lap
13.	Mazzacane	Minardi Fondmetal	engine

Tour	Pilote	Equipe	Motif d'abandon
1	Diniz	Sauber Petronas	accident
1	Heidfeld	Prost Peugeot	accrochage
1	de la Rosa	Arrows	accident
8	Frentzen	Jordan Mugen Honda	steering
19	Button	Williams BMW	oil pump
37	Gené	Minardi Fondmetal	engine
44	R. Schum.	Williams BMW	engine
47	Zonta	BAR Honda	engine
47	Herbert	Jaguar	suspension

FASTEST LAPS

	Drivers	Time	Lap
1.	Häkkinen	1'38"543	34
2.	M. Schum.	1'39"064	21
3.	Barrichello	1'39"302	23
4.	Coulthard	1'39"529	36
5.	Villeneuve	1'40"160	20
6.	Irvine	1'40"292	18
7.	Wurz	1'40"312	19
8.	Zonta	1'40"498	21
9.	Herbert	1'40"764	27
10.	Salo	1'40"896	14
11.	Fisichella	1'40"925	53
12.	Verstappen	1'41"104	27
13.	Trulli	1'41"262	33
14.	Alesi	1'41"634	34
15.	R. Schum.	1'41"729	42
16.	Gené	1'41"928	27
17.	Button	1'42"226	17
18.	Mazzacane	1'43"147	24
19.	Frentzen	1'44"557	3

All results :
© 2000 Fédération Internationale de l'Automobile, 2, Ch. Blandonnet, 1215 Genève 15, Suisse

LAP CHART

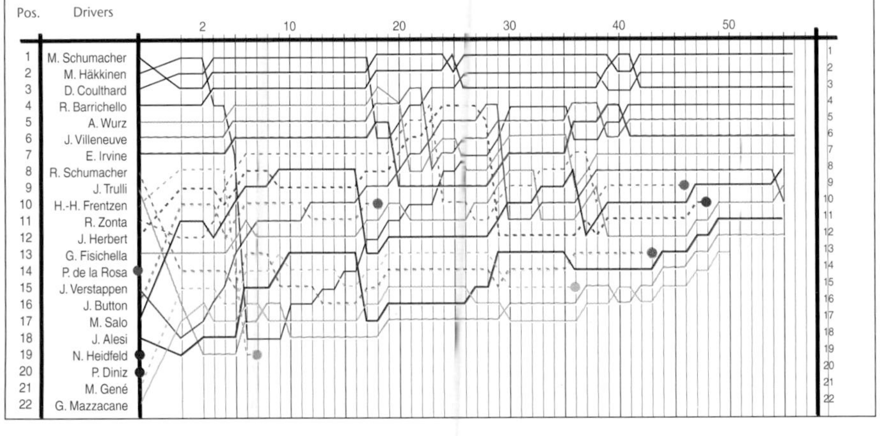
Pos.
Drivers
2
10
20
30
40
50
M. Schumacher
M. Häkkinen
D. Coulthard
R. Barrichello
A. Wurz
J. Villeneuve
E. Irvine
R. Schumacher
J. Trulli
H.-H. Frentzen
R. Zonta
J. Herbert
G. Fisichella
P. de la Rosa
J. Verstappen
J. Button
M. Salo
J. Alesi
N. Heidfeld
P. Diniz
M. Gené
G. Mazzacane

PIT STOPS

	Drivers	Time	Lap	Stop n°
1.	Trulli	40"330	1	1
2.	Häkkinen	37"930	5	1
3.	Frentzen	36"793	6	1
4.	Trulli	37"549	10	2
5.	Salo	35"441	16	1
6.	Alesi	34"902	16	1
7.	Coulthard	33"795	17	1
8.	Irvine	35"143	19	1
9.	Wurz	32"904	20	1
10.	Villeneuve	34"329	22	1
11.	Zonta	33"888	23	1
12.	M. Schum.	33"787	24	1
13.	Barrichello	33"605	25	1
14.	Mazzacane	38"651	27	1
15.	Herbert	50"020	28	1
16.	Gené	38"810	28	1
17.	R. Schum.	38"812	28	1
18.	Verstappen	37"363	29	1
19.	Fisichella	36"041	32	1
20.	Häkkinen	35"470	35	2
21.	Wurz	35"401	35	2
22.	Alesi	35"124	35	2
23.	Salo	35"705	36	2
24.	Zonta	34"930	37	2
25.	Coulthard	33"932	38	2
26.	Villeneuve	35"145	38	2
27.	M. Schum.	32"952	39	2
28.	Trulli	35"229	39	3
29.	Irvine	34"322	40	2
30.	Barrichello	36"349	41	2
31.	Mazzacane	33"255	45	2

BRIDGESTONE

Quickest pit stop during the Malaysian Grand Prix, fitting four new Bridgestone tyres:

Alexander Wurz, Benetton, 32"904

CHAMPIONSHIP

(after eighteen rounds)

Drivers :

1.	M. Schumacher	108
2.	M. Häkkinen	89
3.	D. Coulthard	73
4.	R. Barrichello	62
5.	R. Schumacher	24
6.	G. Fisichella	18
7.	J. Villeneuve	17
8.	J. Button	12
9.	H.-H. Frentzen	11
10.	J. Trulli	6
	M. Salo	6
12.	J. Verstappen	5
13.	E. Irvine	4
14.	R. Zonta	3
15.	A. Wurz	2
	P. de la Rosa	2

Constructors :

1.	Ferrari	170
2.	McLaren Mercedes	152
3.	Williams BMW	36
4.	Benetton Playlife	20
	BAR Honda	20
6.	Jordan Mugen Honda	17
7.	Arrows	7
8.	Sauber Petronas	6
9.	Jaguar	4

THE CIRCUIT

SEVENTEENTH ROUND

PETRONAS MALAYSIAN GRAND PRIX, KUALA LUMPUR

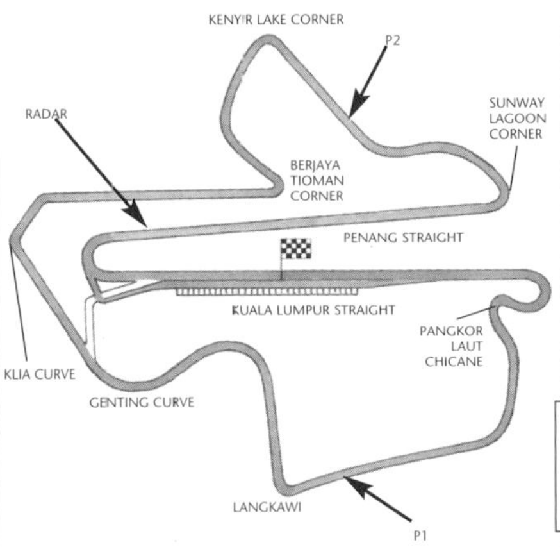
KENYIR LAKE CORNER
P2
SUNWAY LAGOON CORNER
RADAR
BERJAYA TIOMAN CORNER
PENANG STRAIGHT
KUALA LUMPUR STRAIGHT
PANGKOR LAUT CHICANE
KLIA CURVE
GENTING CURVE
LANGKAWI
P1

Date : October 22, 2000
Length : 5542 meters
Distance : 56 laps, 310.408 km
Weather : nice & sunny, 33°

RACE SUMMARY

- Mika Hakkinen makes the best start, while David Coulthard squeezes Michael Schumacher out wide. At the second corner, Diniz runs into the back of Alesi's Prost and Heidfeld hits De La Rosa. The Safety Car comes out while the wrecks are cleared away.
- David Coulthard, Michael Schumacher and Rubens Barrichello pass Hakkinen, who knows he will be brought in for a penalty after jumping the start.
- On lap 10, Coulthard leads Michael Schumacher by 4.8 seconds.
- The Scotsman is the first to pit on lap 20. Schumacher steps up the pace and comes out in the lead after his pit stop. Coulthard chases him all the way to the flag, without managing to get past.

WEEKEND GOSSIP

- **A busy week for Sauber**

The Sauber team had a particularly busy week in Malaysia. With the team's title sponsor, Petronas, being based in Malaysia, the team had to take part in all sorts of public relations exercises. That was why the two drivers came to be driving their C19s through the streets of Penang. "It was good fun," said Pedro Diniz. *"The roads were very dirty and the car was sliding all over the place. It was like a rally crowd, with people on the edge of the road and you had to be very careful not to drive into anyone."* It was here that Peter Sauber dropped a heavy hint about his 2001 driver line-up, which would see the young Finn, Kimi Raikkonen partnering Nick Heidfeld. *"We were very impressed with Kimi's lap times at the last test session. I think we will be making a decision to sign him up soon."*

- **The train is more dangerous than the plane**

Robert Alcorn, who was Mika Hakkinen's personal pilot, was killed in a train crash to the north of London in the week before the grand prix.

- **Telefonica quits**

Telefonica, the Spanish telecom company and Minardi sponsor, announced it would be withdrawing from F1. In Sepang, Giancarlo Minardi said this decision would not have much of an effect on his team and that he was, *"on the point of signing an engine deal for 2001."*

- **Bye bye Johnny**

On Friday, Jaguar hosted a big bash to say farewell to Johnny Herbert, whose Formula 1 career came to an end on race-day. *"If you think I'm going to cry because I'm leaving, you're wrong,"* joked Johnny. *"I think I'll enjoy watching the grands prix from an armchair, with a dog and a drink by my side."*

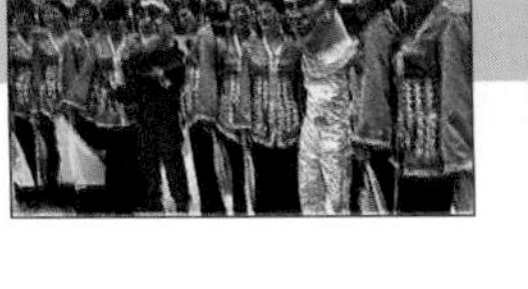

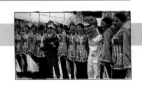

by Pascal Dro

Button-Montoya: the future of F1 is here already

A nice guy who learns very quickly. A driver with no sense of arrogance who lets his performance on the track speak for him. The description applies to two young men who are likely to light up the 2001 season. They both belong to Williams. One is coming back after having been rented out for the past two years to the Chip Ganassi team in the States, while the other is being farmed out on loan, to complete his education with Benetton. For Jenson Button, the target is very clear. He has scored points in six races in 2000 and that after just four seasons of racing cars. Now, his next goal must be that first Formula 1 win. Benetton has not won a race, since

Gerhard Berger did it for them in the German GP, the year he retired. Will a new revitalised Benetton-Renault provide Button with the weapon he and the team needs?

Then we have Juan-Pablo Montoya. He has a steeper mountain to climb, because he will be expected to get on the podium and win races for Williams, without the benefit of a running-in year. Having said that, he already has thousands of F1 miles under his belt, from his days as Williams test driver and he is a CART champion. Montoya seems to have the uncanny ability to adapt in a nanosecond to any car, any track, any discipline. He won his first ever CART

race for example. Naturally, there are comparisons to be made with Jacques Villeneuve, who took a similar route to F1, but the Canadian had it easy, in that he was sitting in the cockpit of the best car on the grid.

Both Button and Montoya will be the centre of attention in 2001. Under 25, they will soon be kicking the established order where it hurts. Even established youngsters like Giancarlo Fisichella and Ralf Schumacher will have to look to their laurels. Button's love of life, Montoya's daring passing moves (maybe) will certainly fill the pages of the newspapers. Roll on the month of March.

▷ The entire Scuderia Ferrari family turns out for the family photo. With two consecutive Constructors' Championships under their belt, Ferrari will come out fighting in 2001.

Williams-BMW en outsiders

Jenson Button had a great debut season in F1. Now he will continue to learn his craft with Benetton, before returning to Williams a fully fledged pro.

▽

More of the same in 2001? *by Luc Domenjoz*

"I think we ended the 2000 season on a positive note. That's good, because it means we should start next season in the same vein," was Rubens Barrichello's point of view after the Malaysian Grand Prix. The Ferrari versus McLaren duel seems to have been going on for ever. Actually, their first confrontation only goes back as far as 1998. Before that, it was Williams who held the high ground and prior to that it was Benetton.

There is a train of thought in Formula 1 that says a team's winning cycle lasts from two to five years. Past experience shows that winning teams inevitably slip back into the pack to be replaced by others on the way up. Will that be the case in 2001? After three years of grey and red domination, another colour on the podium would make a welcome change. In Kuala Lumpur, with the Drivers' title already decided, the future was the main talking point. "Naturally, in 2001, we will have a new car, a new engine and a very strong team," was Jean Todt's take on the situation. "But that does not mean it will be

enough to beat McLaren and Mercedes. Having said that, the Williams-BMW team has progressed a lot this year. I reckon it will be the team to watch next season."

The Williams team actually holds the key to the most interesting driver change. Despite doing remarkably well, Jenson Button will be replaced by the Colombian, Juan-Pablo Montoya, making the move from the American Cart series. Frank Williams is hoping he will not repeat the mistake he made with Alessandro Zanardi, who came from the same discipline. Montoya has a strong background as an F1 test driver and a competitor in Formula 3000.

Jenson Button remains under contract to Williams, while he is "loaned" to Benetton,

where he replaces Alexander Wurz. The Austrian is moving off the grid, to replace Olivier Panis as the third driver in the McLaren camp. As for the Frenchman, he moves back to active competition, partnering Jacques Villeneuve at BAR.

The final driver change of note: Nick Heidfeld has left Prost to go to Sauber. The Swiss team says farewell to both its 2000 drivers; Mika Salo will test for Toyota and Pedro Diniz moves to Prost.

There are no changes at Ferrari, McLaren or Jordan, with these teams banking on stability, always an important element in a successful team. Mika Hakkinen secures his place in the record books as he lines up for his eighth season with the Woking-based outfit.

By a nose! The 2001 cars will not look too different to their predecessors, at least from the front.

▽

Michelin and others

There will be several other changes in 2001, apart from drivers switching cockpits. The vital area of tyres in F1 is about to be turned upside down with Michelin entering the arena after a 16 year absence to end Bridgestone's monopoly. The tyre war will be on again for the first time in two years.

Michelin cannot expect too much from 2001. Bridgestone has a firm contract with the two top teams, Ferrari and McLaren, which should see it take most of the wins and both championships. With Jaguar and Williams already on the books, and others likely to follow during the course of the winter, notably, Benetton and

Prost, Bibendum has an outside chance of picking up the odd win when their tyres are better suited to some of the tracks. "As always with tyres, there will be some circuits where our product will be very good and others where it will not be quite on the pace," commented Michelin's competition boss, Pierre Dupasquier. The tyre war could be yet another plus point for the Williams-BMW team next season. If the French tyres from Clermont Ferrand prove up to the job, then Michelin will no doubt hope to pick up one of the top teams for 2002. Then we can add a contract war to the tyre one.

Prost Grand Prix: make or break

It was an annus horribilis for the French team. Far and away the worst in its twenty five year history, with not a single point to its credit and rock bottom in the Constructors' table. It is all the more unbelievable because of the status of the team and its leader, its technological strengths and the "on paper" status of its staff. It is difficult to unravel the mystery of just what went so catastrophically wrong. The running sore which was the team's relationship with engine supplier Peugeot is not, on its own, good enough cause.

The team accused the car company of supplying an underpowered, unreliable engine, while Peugeot, desperate to get out of the relationship, blamed the poor performance of the AP03 chassis. The result of all this bickering is that it could take longer to rebuild the team's image than to produce a decent technical package. According to rival teams and engine suppliers, the whole package was to blame. It was not even up to Minardi standards. Leaving aside the in-fighting and the turmoil, where does that leave Prost Grand Prix today? A good team that lacks polish, similar to the situation Arrows was in a couple of years back. The English team was running on empty, but it turned itself around in the space of one winter, thanks largely to the arrival of the Supertec engine. Tom Walkinshaw had nurtured hopes that this deal would lead to a works contract with Renault. The irony of the situation is that the very same Walkinshaw will now be running the Peugeot engines, albeit under the Asian Motor Technologies banner. Nevertheless, Arrows managed to beat Sauber to seventh place in the Constructors' Championship in 2000. As for Prost GP, it will switch to the Ferrari 049C V10 which powered Ferrari to the titles

△ Jean Todt and Alain Prost shake hands during their hastily convened press conference in Indianapolis. A new era dawns for the Prost Grand Prix team.

this year. As soon as testing gets underway for 2001, there will be all sorts of interesting questions raised. How will the Peugeot work out in the back of the Arrows? What will the Prost AP04 do with Ferrari power? But most of all, what future awaits the Prost team, which everyone wants to succeed, even if it seems intent on self-destruction? We are looking at the bottom end of the grid here and Arrows, Minardi, Prost and Sauber will have to tough it out against the seven other fully works supported teams. They are no doubt hoping that the major manufacturers will

change policy and decide to supply two teams. One would have thought that, of all of them, the four times World Champion Alain Prost would have been capable of attracting a major constructor. In 2001, the fourth car to bear his name will have to advertise his competence to run a front line team. Next year will be crunch time. Everyone in the Guyancourt factory is aware that if they do not succeed this time, then Alain Prost's reputation as one of the greatest racers of all time will be buried under his failure as a team owner.

Where have all the stars gone?

What will F1 be like in the future? What do future championships have in store for us? These are the questions that crop up every winter. One subject which crops up ever more frequently in magazines and is discussed in pubs and clubs around the land is the fact that, more often than not, victory depends on what happens in the pits. Race wins seem to come down to strategies which are difficult for the man in the street to understand, where a driver is lying second and suddenly, for no apparent reason he is promoted to winner.

The specialists of course, know exactly what is going on, whereas for the casual observer it is getting harder by the day to "read" the race. This means the sport is becoming less and less of a spectacle. These days, the only really exciting part of the races is the start and the finishing order.

Most people regret the passing of a different era, when cars left the line on full tanks and the driver had at least an 80% hold over his own destiny. The sport had an intellectual integrity back then, which has now flown over the pit wall, whereas one used to be able to work out exactly what was going on. This is a

worrying trend, even if the television audience for the sport is growing in spectacular fashion, because those watching at home or in the grandstands will not endure the current trend for much longer.

In future, the drivers will gradually lose their star status and there are already some teams who do not like their drivers to shine like diamonds, preferring anonymous conformity to the party line. It is one of the reasons why Mercedes has now given up on the idea of ever having Michael Schumacher driving for its team. It was also one of the reasons provided by Renault for not supplying Alain Prost with its engines.

The ideal situation for a manufacturer is that its team wins races and titles, without a star driver diverting attention from the team as a whole. Mika Hakkinen is the ultimate example of a team driver, whereas Fiat and Philip Morris must be wondering whether it is Ferrari or Michael Schumacher who walks away with the bulk of the plaudits and publicity. It is the drivers who have made Formula 1 a glamorous pastime and it is the glamour which makes the sport so popular. It might be that in

the future, F1 becomes the contest between nations that it was, even before the world championship was established in 1950. We could have Honda and Toyota representing the Far East, BMW, Mercedes and maybe Audi, if it decides to join the party, representing Germany, Renault and Fiat for the rest of Europe and Ford and General Motors representing the United States. It might be hard to maintain public interest in this sort of contest. When Michael Schumacher first joined the F1 circus, we had Mansell, Piquet, Prost and Senna, slugging it out on the tracks. But when Schumacher goes, who will be left to shine brightly in the minds of the public? Villeneuve, Hakkinen and Coulthard will be past it by then and it will not be easy to replace them with the likes of Honda or Renault.

The tyre truce has ended. In 2001, Michelin will be back on the tracks after a 16 year absence. In 2000, Michelin competition boss Pierre Dupasquier was already spotted on several occasions in the paddock, seeing how the land lies.

▽

Recap of the 2000 season

Pos	Driver	Team	AUS	BRA	RSM	GB	ESP	EUR	MON	CAN	FRA	AUT	GER	HUN	BEL	ITA	USA	JAP	MAL	Poles	Wins	FL	Laps led	Km led	Final
1	Michael SCHUMACHER	Ferrari	1	1	1	3	5	1	A	1	A	A	A	2	2	1	1	1	1	9	9	2	548	2589	108
2	Mika HÄKKINEN	McLaren Mercedes	A	A	2	1	2	6	4	2	1	2	1	1	2	A	2	A	A	5	4	9	352	1750	89
3	David COULTHARD	McLaren Mercedes	A	D	3	1	2	3	1	7	1	3	3	4	A	5	3	2	2	2	3	3	107	479	73
4	Rubens BARRICHELLO	Ferrari	2	A	4	A	3	4	2	2	3	3	1	4	A	A	2	4	3	1	1	3	58	308	62
5	Ralf SCHUMACHER	Williams BMW	3	5	A	4	4	A	14	5	A	7	5	3	3	A	A			-	-	-	-	-	24
6	Giancarlo FISICHELLA	Benetton Playlife	5	2	11	7	9	5	3	3	9	A	A	A	11	A	14	9		-	-	-	-	-	18
7	Jacques VILLENEUVE	BAR Honda	4	A	5	16	A	A	7	15	4	4	8	12	7	A	4	6	5	-	-	-	-	-	17
8	Jenson BUTTON	Williams BMW	A	6	A	5	17	10	A	11	8	5	4	9	5	A	5	A		-	-	-	-	-	12
9	Heinz-Harald FRENTZEN	Jordan Mugen Honda	A	3	A	17	6	A	10	A	7	A	A	6	6	A	3	A	A	-	-	-	9	47	11
10	Jarno TRULLI	Jordan Mugen Honda	A	4	15	6	12	A	6	6	A	9	7	A	13	12				-	-	-	-	-	6
11	Mika SALO	Sauber Petronas	D	F	6	8	7	A	5	10	6	5	10	9	7	A	10	8		-	-	-	-	-	6
12	Jos VERSTAPPEN	Arrows	A	7	14	A	A	A	5	A	4	A	13	15	4	A	10			-	-	-	-	-	5
13	Eddie IRVINE	Jaguar	A	A	7	13	11	A	4	13	13	F	10	8	10	A	7	8	6	-	-	-	-	-	4
14	Ricardo ZONTA	BAR Honda	6	9	12	A	8	A	8	A	A	14	12	6	6	9	A			-	-	-	-	-	3
15	Alexander WURZ	Benetton Playlife	7	A	9	9	10	12	A	9	A	10	A	11	13	5	10	A	7	-	-	-	-	-	2
16	Pedro de la ROSA	Arrows	A	8	A	A	6	A	A	A	6	16	16	A	12	A				-	-	-	-	-	2

Then by alphabetical order:

	Driver	Team	AUS	BRA	RSM	GB	ESP	EUR	MON	CAN	FRA	AUT	GER	HUN	BEL	ITA	USA	JAP	MAL
	Jean ALESI	Prost Peugeot	A	A	10	A	9	A	A	14	A	A	A	12	A	A	11		
	Pedro DINIZ	Sauber Petronas	A	F	8	11	A	7	A	10	11	9	A	A	11	8	8	11	A
	Marc GENÉ	Minardi Fondmetal	8	A	A	14	14	A	16	15	8	A	15	14	9	12	A	A	
	Nick HEIDFELD	Prost Peugeot	9	A	A	16	D	8	A	12	A	12	A	A	9	A	A	A	
	Johnny HERBERT	Jaguar	A	A	10	12	13	11	9	A	A	7	A	8	A	11	7	A	
	Gaston MAZZACANE	Minardi Fondmetal	A	10	13	14	15	8	A	12	A	12	11	A	17	10	A	15	13
	Luciano BURTI	Jaguar									11								

Nber of poles

Senna	65
Prost	33
Clark	33
Mansell	32
M. Schumacher	32
Fangio	28
Häkkinen	26
Lauda	24
Piquet	24
D. Hill	20
Andretti	18
Arnoux	18
Stewart	17
Moss	16
Ascari	14
Hunt	14
Peterson	14
Brabham	13
G. Hill	13
Ickx	13
J. Villeneuve	13
Berger	12
Rindt	10
Coulthard	10
Surtees	8
Patrese	8
Laffite	7
Fittipaldi	6
P. Hill	6
Jabouille	6
Jones	6
Reutemann	6
Amon	5
Farina	5
Regazzoni	5
Rosberg	5
Tambay	5
Hawthorn	4
Pironi	4
De Angelis	3
Brooks	3
T. Fabi	3
Gonzales	3
Gurney	3
Jarier	3
Scheckter	3
Barrichello	3
Then :	
Alesi	2
Frentzen	2
Fisichella	1

Nber of victories

Prost	51
M. Schumacher	44
Senna	41
Mansell	31
Stewart	27
Clark	25
Lauda	25
Fangio	24
Piquet	23
D. Hill	22
Häkkinen	18
Moss	16
Brabham	14
Fittipaldi	14
G. Hill	14
Ascari	13
Andretti	12
Jones	12
Reutemann	12
J. Villeneuve	11
Hunt	10
Peterson	10
Scheckter	10
Berger	10
Coulthard	9
Hulme	8
Ickx	8
Arnoux	7
Brooks	6
Laffite	6
Rindt	6
Surtees	6
G. Villeneuve	6
Patrese	6
Alboreto	5
Farina	5
Regazzoni	5
Rosberg	5
Watson	5
Gurney	4
McLaren	4
Boutsen	3
P. Hill	3
Hawthorn	3
Pironi	3
Irvine	3
Frentzen	3
Herbert	3
Then :	
Panis	1
Alesi	1
Barrichello	1

Number of fastest laps

Prost	41
M. Schumacher	41
Mansell	30
Clark	28
Lauda	25
Fangio	23
Piquet	23
Berger	21
Häkkinen	21
Moss	20
D. Hill	19
Senna	19
Regazzoni	15
Stewart	15
Ickx	14
Coulthard	14
Jones	13
Patrese	13
Arnoux	12
Ascari	11
Surtees	11
Andretti	10
Brabham	10
G. Hill	10
Hulme	9
Peterson	9
J. Villeneuve	9
Hunt	8
Laffite	7
G. Villeneuve	7
Farina	6
Fittipaldi	6
Gonzalez	6
Gurney	6
Hawthorn	6
P. Hill	6
Pironi	6
Scheckter	6
Frentzen	6
Pace	5
Watson	5
Alesi	4
Alboreto	4
Beltoise	4
Depailler	4
Reutemann	4
Siffert	4
Barrichello	3
Then :	
Wurz	1
Irvine	1
R.Schumacher	1

Total number of points scored

Prost	798.5
M. Schumacher	678
Senna	614
Piquet	485.5
Mansell	482
Lauda	420.5
Berger	386
Häkkinen	383
Stewart	360
D. Hill	360
Reutemann	310
Coulthard	294
G. Hill	289
E. Fittipaldi	281
Patrese	281
Fangio	277.5
Clark	274
Brabham	261
Scheckter	259
Alesi	236
Laffite	228
Regazzoni	212
Jones	206
Peterson	206
J. Villeneuve	197
McLaren	196.5
Alboreto	186.5
Moss	186.5
Arnoux	181
Ickx	181
Ma. Andretti	180
Surtees	180
Hunt	179
Irvine	177
Watson	169
Frentzen	153
Barrichello	139
Then :	
Herbert	98
R. Schumacher	86
Fisichella	67
Panis	56
Salo	31
Wurz	26
Trulli	17
Button	12
Diniz	10
de la Rosa	3
Zonta	3
Gené	1

Nber of laps in the lead

Senna	2'999
Prost	2'705
M. Schumacher	2'560
Mansell	2'099
Clark	2'039
Stewart	1'893
Lauda	1'620
Piquet	1'572
Häkkinen	1'376
D. Hill	1'352
G. Hill	1'073
Brabham	827
Andretti	799
Peterson	706
Berger	695
Coulthard	682
Scheckter	671
Reutemann	648
Hunt	634
J. Villeneuve	634
Jones	594
Patrese	568
G. Villeneuve	533
Ickx	529
Arnoux	506
Rosberg	506
Fittipaldi	459
Hulme	436
Rindt	387
Regazzoni	361
Surtees	310
Pironi	295
Watson	287
Laffite	279
Alesi	271
Alboreto	218
Tambay	197
Gurney	191
P. Hill	189
Jabouille	184
Amon	183
Brooks	173
Depailler	165
Irvine	156
Frentzen	149
Barrichello	129
Then :	
Herbert	44
Trulli	37
Fisichella	35
Panis	16
R. Schumacher	8
Salo	2

Nber of km in the lead

Senna	13'613
Prost	12'575
M. Schumacher	11'789
Clark	10'189
Mansell	9'642
Stewart	9'077
Piquet	7'465
Lauda	7'188
Häkkinen	6'653
D. Hill	6'248
G. Hill	4'618
Brabham	4'541
Andretti	3'577
Berger	3'456
Coulthard	3'313
Reutemann	3'309
Peterson	3'304
Hunt	3'229
Ickx	3'067
J. Villeneuve	2'972
Jones	2'877
Scheckter	2'837
Patrese	2'571
Arnoux	2'561
G. Villeneuve	2'244
Rosberg	2'137
Surtees	2'131
Fittipaldi	2'122
Rindt	1'905
Hulme	1'900
Regazzoni	1'855
P. Hill	1'715
Brooks	1'525
Gurney	1'518
Laffite	1'476
Alesi	1'297
Watson	1'245
Pironi	1'238
Jabouille	978
Tambay	975
Alboreto	927
Irvine	838
Von Trips	787
Amon	784
Frentzen	745
Barrichello	393
Then :	
Herbert	226
Fisichella	172
Trulli	160
Panis	53
R. Schumacher	36
Salo	13

Nber of GP contested

Patrese	256
Berger	210
DeCesaris	208
Piquet	204
Prost	199
Alboreto	194
Mansell	187
Alesi	183
G. Hill	176
Laffite	176
Lauda	171
Boutsen	163
Herbert	162
Senna	161
Brundle	158
Watson	152
Arnoux	149
Warwick	147
Reutemann	146
M. Schum.	145
Häkkinen	145
E. Fittipaldi	144
Jarier	135
Cheever	132
Regazzoni	132
Barrichello	130
Ma. Andretti	128
Brabham	126
Peterson	123
Martini	119
Ickx	116
Jones	116
D. Hill	116
Rosberg	114
Tambay	114
Frentzen	114
Irvine	113
Hulme	112
Scheckter	112
Surtees	111
De Angelis	108
Alliot	107
Coulthard	107
Mass	105
Bonnier	102
McLaren	101
Stewart	99
Diniz	98
Siffert	97
Amon	96
Depailler	95
Katayama	95
Capelli	94
Salo	93
Hunt	92
Panis	91
Beltoise	86
Gurney	86
Palmer	84
Surer	82
Trintignant	82
J. Villeneuve	82
Johansson	79
Nannini	77
Ghinzani	76
Nakajima	74
Brambilla	74
Gugelmin	74
Stuck	74
Fisichella	74
Clark	72
Pace	72
Modena	70
Pironi	70
Then :	
R. Schumacher	65
Trulli	61
Badoer	50
Wurz	52
Zanardi	41
Gené	32
Takagi	31

Abbreviations : A = retired; NQ = not qualified; DNF = not finished; F = forfeit; D = disqualified; NC = finished, but not classified (insufficient distance covered); ARG = Argentina; AUS = Australia; AUT = Autria; BEL = Belgique; BRE = Brésil; CAN = Canada; DAL = Dallas; ESP = Espagne; EUR = Europe; FIN = Finland; FRA = France; GB = England; GER = Germany HOL = The Netherlands; ITA = Italy; JAP = Japon; MEX = Mexico; MON = Monaco; NZ = New-Zealand; PAC = Pacific; POR = Portugal; RSM = San-Marino; SA = South Africa; SUE = Sweden; SUI = Switzerland; USA = Etats-Unis;USAE = East USA ; USAW = West USA; VEG = Las Vegas; NB = Laps in the lead only since 1957.

The 51 World Champions

Year	Driver	Nationality	Make	Nber of races	Nber of poles	Nber of victories	Nber of fastest laps
1950	Giuseppe Farina	ITA	Alfa Romèo	7	2	3	3
1951	Juan Manuel Fangio	ARG	Alfa Romèo	8	4	3	5
1952	Alberto Ascari	ITA	Ferrari	8	5	6	5
1953	Alberto Ascari	ITA	Ferrari	9	6	5	5
1954	Juan Manuel Fangio	ARG	Mercedes/Maserati	9	5	6	3
1955	Juan Manuel Fangio	ARG	Mercedes	7	3	4	3
1956	Juan Manuel Fangio	ARG	Lancia/Ferrari	8	5	3	3
1957	Juan Manuel Fangio	ARG	Maserati	8	4	4	2
1958	Mike Hawthorn	GB	Ferrari	11	4	1	5
1959	Jack Brabham	AUS	Cooper Climax	9	1	2	1
1960	Jack Brabham	AUS	Cooper Climax	10	3	5	3
1961	Phil Hill	USA	Ferrari	8	5	2	2
1962	Graham Hill	GB	BRM	9	1	4	3
1963	Jim Clark	GB	Lotus Climax	10	7	7	6
1964	John Surtees	GB	Ferrari	10	2	2	2
1965	Jim Clark	GB	Lotus Climax	10	6	6	6
1966	Jack Brabham	AUS	Brabham Repco	9	3	4	1
1967	Dennis Hulme	NZ	Brabham Repco	11	0	2	2
1968	Graham Hill	GB	Lotus Ford	12	2	3	0
1969	Jackie Stewart	GB	Matra Ford	11	2	6	5
1970	Jochen Rindt	AUT	Lotus Ford	13	3	5	1
1971	Jackie Stewart	GB	Matra Ford	11	6	6	3
1972	Emerson Fittipaldi	BRE	Lotus Ford	12	3	5	0
1973	Jackie Stewart	GB	Tyrrell Ford	15	3	5	1
1974	Emerson Fittipaldi	BRE	McLaren Ford	15	2	3	0
1975	Niki Lauda	AUT	Ferrari	14	9	5	2
1976	James Hunt	GB	McLaren Ford	16	8	6	2
1977	Niki Lauda	AUT	Ferrari	17	2	3	3
1978	Mario Andretti	USA	Lotus Ford	16	8	6	3
1979	Jody Scheckter	SA	Ferrari	15	1	3	1
1980	Alan Jones	AUS	Williams Ford	14	3	5	5
1981	Nelson Piquet	BRE	Brabham Ford	15	4	3	1
1982	Keke Rosberg	FIN	Williams Ford	16	1	1	0
1983	Nelson Piquet	BRE	Brabham BMW Turbo	15	1	3	4
1984	Niki Lauda	AUT	McLaren TAG Porsche Turbo	16	0	5	5
1985	Alain Prost	FRA	McLaren TAG Porsche Turbo	16	2	5	5
1986	Alain Prost	FRA	McLaren TAG Porsche Turbo	16	1	4	2
1987	Nelson Piquet	BRE	Williams Honda Turbo	16	4	3	4
1988	Ayrton Senna	BRE	McLaren Honda Turbo	16	13	8	3
1989	Alain Prost	FRA	McLaren Honda	16	2	4	5
1990	Ayrton Senna	BRE	McLaren Honda	16	10	6	2
1991	Ayrton Senna	BRE	McLaren Honda	16	8	7	2
1992	Nigel Mansell	GB	Williams Renault	16	14	9	8
1993	Alain Prost	FRA	Williams Renault	16	13	7	6
1994	Michael Schumacher	GER	Benetton Ford	14	6	8	9
1995	Michael Schumacher	GER	Benetton Renault	17	4	9	7
1996	Damon Hill	GB	Williams Renault	16	9	8	5
1997	Jacques Villeneuve	CAN	Williams Renault	17	10	7	3
1998	Mika Häkkinen	FIN	McLaren Mercedes	16	9	8	6
1999	Mika Häkkinen	FIN	McLaren Mercedes	16	11	5	6
2000	Michael Schumacher	GER	Ferrari	17	9	9	2

Constructor's championship 2000

Position	Team	Nber of points	Nber of poles	Nber of victories	Nber fastest laps	Nber laps in lead	Nber km. in lead
1.	Ferrari	170	10	10	5	606	2898
2.	McLaren Mercedes	152	7	7	12	459	2229
3.	Williams BMW	36	0	0	0	0	0
4.	Benetton Playlife	20	0	0	0	0	0
5.	BAR Honda	20	0	0	0	0	0
6.	Jordan Mugen Honda	17	0	0	0	9	47
7.	Arrows	7	0	0	0	0	0
8.	Sauber Petronas	6	0	0	0	0	0
9.	Jaguar	4	0	0	0	0	0
10.	Minardi Fondmetal	0	0	0	0	0	0
11.	Prost Peugeot	0	0	0	0	0	0

Nber of constructor's championship titles
(exists since 1958)

10 : Ferrari
1961 - 64 - 75 - 76 - 77 - 79 - 82 - 83 - 99 - 2000

9 : Williams
1980 - 81 - 86 - 87 -92 - 93 - 94 - 96 - 97

8 : McLaren
1974 - 84 - 85 - 88 - 89 - 90 - 91 - 98

7 : Lotus
1963 - 65 - 68 - 70 -72 - 73 - 78

2 : Cooper 1959 - 60
Brabham 1966 - 67

1 : Vanwall 1958
BRM 1962
Matra 1969
Tyrrell 1971
Benetton 1995

Number of poles per make

Ferrari	137
Williams	108
Lotus	107
McLaren	110
Brabham	39
Renault	31
Benetton	16
Tyrrell	14
Alfa Romèo	12
BRM	11
Cooper	11
Maserati	10
Ligier	9
Mercedes	8
Vanwall	7
March	5
Matra	4
Shadow	3
Lancia	2
Jordan	2
Arrows	1
Honda	1
Lola	1
Porsche	1
Wolf	1
Stewart	1

Nber of victories per make

Ferrari	135
McLaren	130
Williams	103
Lotus	79
Brabham	35
Benetton	26
Tyrrell	23
BRM	17
Cooper	16
Renault	1
Alfa Romèo	10
Maserati	9
Matra	9
Mercedes	9
Vanwall	9
Ligier	9
March	3
Wolf	3
Jordan	3
Honda	2
Hesketh	1
Penske	1
Porsche	1
Shadow	1
Stewart	1

Nber of fastest laps per make

Ferrari	144
Williams	110
McLaren	92
Lotus	70
Brabham	41
Benetton	37
Tyrrell	20
Renault	18
BRM	15
Maserati	15
Alfa Romèo	14
Cooper	13
Matra	12
Ligier	11
Mercedes	9
March	7
Vanwall	6
Surtees	4
Eagle	2
Honda	2
Shadow	2
Wolf	2
Ensign	1
Gordini	1
Hesketh	1
Lancia	1
Parnelli	1
Jordan	1

Family picture of the 2000 championship. From left to right and from top to bottom: Pedro Diniz, Mika Salo, Ralf Schumacher, Eddie Irvine, Johnny Herbert, Jos Verstappen, Pedro de la Rosa, Jacques Villeneuve, Ricardo Zonta, Heinz-Harald Frentzen, Jarno Trulli, Marc Gené, Gaston Mazzacane, Giancarlo Fisichella, Alexander Wurz, David Coulthard, Mika Häkkinen, Michael Schumacher, Rubens Barrichello, Jean Alesi, Nick Heidfeld.

Sporting regulations

The FIA will organise the FIA Formula One World Championship (the Championship) which is the property of the FIA and comprises two titles of World Champion, one for drivers and one for constructors. It consists of the Formula One Grand Prix races which are included in the Formula One calendar and in respect of which the ASNs and organisers have signed the organisation agreement provided for in the 1998 Concorde Agreement (...)

LICENCES

10. All drivers, competitors and officials participating in the Championship must hold a FIA Super Licence. Applications for Super Licences must be made to the FIA through the applicant's ASN.

CHAMPIONSHIP EVENTS

11. Events are reserved for Formula One cars as defined in the Technical Regulations.

12. Each Event will have the status of an international restricted competition.

13. The distance of all races, from the start signal referred to in Article 141 to the chequered flag, shall be equal to the least number of complete laps which exceed a distance of 305 km. However, should two hours elapse before the scheduled race distance is completed, the leader will be shown the chequered flag when he crosses the control line (the Line) at the end of the lap during which the two hour period ended. The Line is a single line which crosses both the track and the pit lane.

14. The maximum number of Events in the Championship is 17, the minimum is 8.

16. An Event which is cancelled with less than three months written notice to the FIA will not be considered for inclusion in the following year's Championship unless the FIA judges the cancellation to have been due to force majeure.

17. An Event may be cancelled if fewer than 12 cars are available for it.

WORLD CHAMPIONSHIP

18) The Formula One World Championship driver's title will be awarded to the driver who has scored the highest number of points, taking into consideration all the results obtained during the Events which have actually taken place.

19. Points will not be awarded for the Championship unless the driver has driven the same car throughout the race in the Event in question.

20. The title of Formula One World Champion for Constructors will be awarded to the make which has scored the highest number of points, taking into account all the results obtained by a maximum of 2 cars per make.

21. The constructor of an engine or rolling chassis is the person (including any corporate or unincorporated body) which owns the intellectual property rights to such engine or chassis. The make of an engine or chassis is the name attributed to it by its constructor. If the make of the chassis is not the same as that of the engine, the title will be awarded to the former which shall always precede the latter in the name of the car.

22. Points for both titles will be awarded at each Event according to the following scale :

1st : 10 points; 2nd : 6 points; 3rd : 4 points; 4th : 3 points; 5th : 2 points; 6th : 1 point.

23. If a race is stopped under Articles 155 and 156, and cannot be restarted, no points will be awarded in case A, half points will be awarded in case B and full points will be awarded in case C.

24. Drivers finishing first, second and third in the Championship must be present at the annual FIA Prize Giving ceremony. Any such driver who is absent will be liable to a maximum fine of US $ 50,000.00. All competitors shall use their best endeavours to ensure that their drivers attend as aforesaid.

DEAD HEAT

25. Prizes and points awarded for all the positions of competitors who tie, will be added together and shared equally.

26. If two or more constructors or drivers finish the season with the same number of points, the higher place in the Championship (in either case) shall be awarded to :

a) the holder of the greatest number of first places,

b) if the number of first places is the same, the holder of the greatest number of second places,

c) if the number of second places is the same, the holder of the greatest number of third places and so on until a winner emerges.

d) if this procedure fails to produce a result, the FIA will nominate the winner according to such criteria as it thinks fit.

COMPETITORS APPLICATIONS

42. Applications to compete in the Championship may be submitted to the FIA at any time between 1 November and 15 November each year, on an entry form as set out in Appendix 2 hereto accompanied by the entry fee provided for in the Agreement. Entry forms will be made available by FIA who will notify the applicant of the result of the application no later than 1 December. Successful applicants are automatically entered in all Events of the Championship and will be the only competitors at Events.

44. A competitor may change the make and/or type of engine at any time during the Championship. All points scored with an engine of different make to that which was first entered in the Championship will count (and will be aggregated) for the assessment of Benefits and for determining team positions for pre-qualifying purposes, however such points will not count towards (nor be aggregated for) the FIA Formula One Constructors Championship.

45. With the exception of those whose cars have scored points in the Championship of the previous year, applicants must supply information about the size of their company, their financial position and their ability to meet their prescribed obligations. All applicants who did not take part in the entire Championship for the previous year must also deposit US$500,000.00 with the FIA when submitting their application. This sum will be returned to them forthwith if their application is refused or at the end of their first Championship season provided they have met all the requirements of the Agreement and its schedules.

46. All applications will be studied by the FIA which will publish the list of cars and drivers accepted together with their race numbers on 1 December (or the following Monday if 1 December falls on a week-end), having first notified unsuccessful applicants as set out in article 42.

47. No more than 24 will be accepted from any one competitor.

INCIDENTS

53. Incident means any occurrence or series of occurrences involving one or more drivers, or any action by any driver, which is reported to the stewards by the race director (or noted by the stewards and referred to the race director for investigation) which :

- necessitated the stopping of a race under Article 155;
- constituted a breach of these Sporting Regulations or the Code;
- caused a false start by one or more cars;
- caused an avoidable collision;
- forced a driver off the track;
- illegitimately prevented a legitimate overtaking manoeuvre by a driver;
- illegitimately impeded another driver during overtaking.

54. a) It shall be at the discretion of the stewards to decide, upon a report or a request by the race director, if a driver or drivers involved in an incident shall be penalised.

b) If an incident is under investigation by the stewards, a message informing all Teams of this will be displayed on the timing monitors.

c) If a driver is involved in a collision or Incident (see Article 53), he must not leave the circuit without the consent of the stewards.

55. The stewards may impose a 10 second time penalty on any driver involved in an Incident. However, should such penalty be imposed during the last five laps, or after the end of a race, Artice 56b) below will not apply and 25 seconds will be added to the elapsed race time of the driver concerned.

56. Should the stewards decide to impose a time penalty, the following procedure will be followed :

a) The stewards will give written notification of the time penalty which has been imposed to an official of the team concerned and will ensure that this information is also displayed on the timing monitors.

b) From the time the steward's decision is notified on the timing monitors the relevant driver may cover no more than three complete laps before entering the pits and proceeding to his pit where he shall remain for the period of the time penalty. During the time the car is stationary for the time penalty it may not be worked on. However, if the engine stops, it may be started after the time penalty period has elapsed.

c) When the time penalty period has elapsed the driver may rejoin the race.

d) Any breach or failure to comply with Articles 56 b) or 56 c) may result in the car being excluded.

57. Any determination made or any penalty imposed pursuant to Article 55 shall be without prejudice to the operation of Articles 160 or 161 of the Code.

PROTESTS

58. Protests shall be made in accordance with the Code and accompanied by a fee of 2500.00 Swiss Francs or its equivalent in US Dollars or local currency.

SANCTIONS

59. The stewards may inflict the penalties specifically set out in these Sporting Regulations in addition to or instead of any other penalties available to them under the Code.

CHANGES OF DRIVER

60. During a season, each team will be permitted one driver change for their first car and will be permitted to have three drivers for their second car who may be changed at any time provided that any driver change is made in accordance with the Code and before the start of qualifying practice. After 18.00 on the day of scrutineering, a driver change may only take place with the consent of the stewards. In all other circumstances, competitors will be obliged to use the drivers they nominated at the time of entering the Championship except in cases of force majeure which will be considered separately. Any new driver may score points in the Championship.

PIT LANE

66. a) For the avoidance of doubt and for description purposes, the pit lane shall be divided into two lanes. The lane closest to the pit wall is designated the "fast lane", and the lane closest to the garages is designated the "inner lane", and is the only area where any work can be carried out on a car.

b) Competitors must not paint lines on any part of the pit lane.

c) No equipment may be left in the fast lane. A car may enter or remain in the fast lane only with the driver sitting in the car behind the steering wheel in his normal position, even when the car is being pushed.

d) Team personnel are only allowed in the pit lane immediately before they are required to work on a car and must withdraw as soon as the work is complete.

e) It is the responsibility of the Competitor to release his car after a pit stop only when it is safe to do so.

SPORTING CHECKS

67. Each competitor must have all relevant Super Licences available for inspection at any time during the Event.

SCRUTINEERING

70. Initial scrutineering of the car will take place three days (Monaco : four days) before the race between 10.00 and 16.00 in the garage assigned to each team.

71. Unless a waiver is granted by the stewards, competitors who do not keep to these time limits will not be allowed to take part in the Event.

72. No car may take part in the Event until it has been passed by the scrutineers.

73. The scrutineers may :

a) check the eligibility of a car or of a competitor at any time during an Event,

b) require a car to be dismantled by the competitor to make sure that the conditions of eligibility or conformity are fully satisfied,

c) require a competitor to pay the reasonable expenses which exercise of the powers mentioned in this Article may entail,

d) require a competitor to supply them with such parts or samples as they may deem necessary.

74. Any car which, after being passed by the scrutineers, is dismantled or modified in a way which might affect its safety or call into question its eligibility, or which is involved in an accident with similar consequences, must be re-presented for scrutineering approval.

75. The race director or the clerk of the course may require that any car involved in an accident be stopped and checked.

77. The stewards will publish the findings of the scrutineers each time cars are checked during the Event. These results will not include any specific figure except when a car is found to be in breach of the Technical Regulations.

SUPPLY OF TYRES IN THE CHAMPIONSHIP AND TYRE LIMITATION DURING THE EVENT

78. Supply of tyres : No tyre may be used in the Championship unless the company supplying such tyre accepts and adheres to the following conditions :

- one tyre supplier present in the Championship: this company must equip 100% of the entered teams on ordinary commercial terms.

- two tyre suppliers present : each of them must, if called upon to do so, be prepared to equip up to 60% of the entered teams on ordinary commercial terms.

- three or more tyre suppliers present : each of them must, if called upon to do so, be prepared to equip up to 40% of the entered teams on ordinary commercial terms.

- each tyre supplier must undertake to provide only two specifications of dry-weather tyre and three specifications of wet-weather tyre at each Event, each of which must be of one homogenous compound only;(...)

79. Quantity and type of tyres :

a) The same driver may not use more than a total of thirty two dry-weather tyres and twenty eight wet-weather tyres throughout the entire duration of the Event. Prior to the qualifying practice each driver may use two specifications of dry-weather tyres but must, before qualifying practice begins, nominate which specification of tyre he will use for the remainder of the Event. For qualifying practice, warm up and the race each driver may use no more than twenty eight tyres (fourteen front and fourteen rear).

b) All dry-weather tyres must incorporate circumferential grooves square to the wheel axis and around the entire circumference of the contact surface of each tyre.

c) Each front dry-weather tyre, when new, must incorporate 4 grooves which are :

- arranged symmetrically about the centre of the tyre tread ;

- at least 14 mm wide at the contact surface and which taper uniformly to a minimum of 10 mm at the lower surface ;

- at least 2.5 mm deep across the whole lower surface ;

- 50 mm (+/- 1.0 mm) between centres.

Furthermore, the tread width of the front tyres must not exceed 270 mm.

d) Each rear dry-weather tyre, when new, must incorporate 4 grooves which are:

- arranged symmetrically about the centre of the tyre tread ;

- at least 14 mm wide at the contact surface and which taper uniformly to a minimum of 10 mm at the lower surface ;

- at least 2.5 mm deep across the whole lower surface ; - 50 mm (+/- 1.0 mm) between centres.

The measurements referred to in c) and d) above will be taken when the tyre is fitted to a wheel and inflated to 20 psi.

e) A wet-weather tyre is one which has been designed for use on a wet or damp track.

All wet-weather tyres must, when new, have a contact area which does not exceed 300 cm? when fitted to the front of the car and 475 cm? when fitted to the rear. Contact areas will be measured over any square section of the tyre which is normal to and symmetrical about the tyre centre line and which measures 200 mm x 200 mm when fitted to the front of the car and 250 mm x 250 mm when fitted to the rear. For the purposes of establishing conformity, only void areas which are greater than 2.5 mm in depth will be considered.

Prior to use at an Event, each tyre manufacturer must provide the technical delegate with a full scale drawing of each type of wet-weather tyre intended for use. With the exception of race day, wet-weather tyres may only be used after the track has been declared wet by the race director and, during the remainder of the relevant session, the choice of tyres is free.

80. Control of tyres :

a) All tyres which are to be used at an Event will be marked with a unique identification.

b) At any time during an Event, and at his absolute discretion, the FIA technical delegate may select the dry-weather tyres to be used by any Team from among the total stock of tyres which such Team's designated supplier has present at the Event.

c) During initial scrutineering, each competitor may have up to forty four dry-weather tyres and thirty six wet-weather tyres for each of his drivers ready for marking in his garage. Tyres not marked during initial scrutineering can be marked at other times by arrangement with the FIA technical delegate.

d) From among the twenty-eight dry-weather tyres chosen for each car for qualifying practice, warm up and the race, the FIA technical delegate will choose at random sixteen tyres (eight front and eight rear) which are the only dry-weather tyres which such car may use in qualifying practice.

e) A competitor wishing to replace an already marked unused tyre by another unused one must present both tyres to the FIA technical delegate.

f) The use of tyres without appropriate identification is strictly forbidden.

81. Wear of tyres :

The Championship will be contested on grooved tyres. The FIA reserve the right to introduce at any time a method of measuring remaining groove depth if performance appears to be enhanced by high wear or by the use of tyres which are worn so that the grooves are no longer visible.

WEIGHING

82. The weight of any car may be checked during the Event as follows :

a) all drivers entered in the Championship will be weighed, wearing their complete racing apparel, at the first Event of the season. If a driver is entered later in the season he will be weighed at his first Event.

b) During qualifying practice :

1) the FIA will install weighing equipment in an area as close to the first pit as possible, this area will be used for the weighing procedure ;

2) cars will be selected at random to undergo the weighing procedure. The FIA technical delegate will inform the driver by means of a red light at the pit entrance that his car has been selected for weighing

3) having been signalled (by means of a red light), that his car has been selected for weighing, the driver will proceed directly to the weighing area and stop his engine ;

4) the car will then be weighed and the result given to the driver in writing ;

5) if the car is unable to reach the weighing area under its own power it will be placed under the exclusive control of the marshals who will take the car to be weighed ;

6) a car or driver may not leave the weighing area without the consent of the FIA technical delegate.

c) After the race :

Each car crossing the Line will be weighed. If a car is weighed without the driver, the weight determined under a) above will be added to give the total weight required under Article 4.1 of the Technical Regulations.

d) Should the weight of the car be less than that specified in Article 4.1 of the Technical Regulations when weighed under b) or c) above, the car and the driver will be excluded from the Event save where the deficiency in weight results from the accidental loss of a component of the car due to force majeure.

e) No solid, liquid, gas or other substance or matter of whatsoever nature may be added to, placed on, or removed from a car after it has been selected for weighing or has finished the race or during the weighing procedure. (...)

f) Only scrutineers and officials may enter the weighing area. No intervention of any kind is allowed there unless authorised by such officials.

83. Any breach of these provisions for the weighing of cars may result in the exclusion of the relevant car.

SPARE CAR

86. A competitor may use several cars for practice and the race provided that :

a) he uses no more than two cars (one car for a one car Team) for free practice sessions on each of the two practice days held under Article 115 a) and b) ;

b) he uses no more than three cars (two cars for a one car Team) during qualifying practice;

c) they are all of the same make and were entered in the Championship by the same competitor,

d) they have been scrutineered in accordance with these Sporting Regulations,

e) each car carries its driver's race number.

87. Changes of car may only take place in the pits under supervision of the marshals.

88. No change of car will be allowed after the green light (see Article 139) provided always that if a race has to be restarted under Article 157 Case A, the moment after which no car change will be allowed shall be when the green light for the subsequent start is shown.

GENERAL SAFETY

90. Drivers are strictly forbidden to drive their car in the opposite direction to the race unless this is absolutely necessary in order to move the car from a dangerous position. A car may only be pushed to remove it from a dangerous position as directed by the marshals.

91. Any driver intending to leave the track or to go to his pit or the paddock area must signal his intention to do so in good time making sure that he can do this without danger.

93. A driver who abandons a car must leave it in neutral or with the clutch disengaged and with the steering wheel in place.

94. Repairs to a car may be carried out only in the paddock, pits and on the grid.

96. Save as provided in Article 138, refuelling is allowed only in the pits.

99. Save as specifically authorised by the Code or these Sporting Regulations, no one except the driver may touch a stopped car unless it is in the pits or on the starting grid.

101. During the periods commencing 15 minutes prior to and ending 5 minutes after every practice session and the period between the green lights being illuminated (Article 139) and the time when the last car enters the parc fermé, no one is allowed on the track with the exception of :

a) marshals or other authorised personnel in the execution of their duty ;

b) drivers when driving or under the direction of the marshals ;

c) mechanics under Article 140 only.

102. During a race, the engine may only be started with the starter except in the pit lane where the use of an external starting device is allowed (...)

104. A speed limit of 80 km/h in practice and 120 km/h during the warm up and the race, or such other speed limits as the Permanent Bureau of the Formula One Commission may decide, will be enforced in the pit lane. Except in the race, any driver who exceeds the limit will be fined US$250 for each km/h above the limit (this may be increased in the case of a second offence in the same Championship season). During the race, the stewards may impose a time penalty on any driver who exceeds the limit.

105. If a driver has serious mechanical difficulties during practice or the race he must leave the track as soon as it is safe to do so.

106. The car's rear light must be illuminated at all times when it is running on wet-weather tyres.

107. Only six team members per participating car (all of whom shall have been issued with and wearing special identification) are allowed in the signalling area during practice and the race.

109. The race director, the clerk of the course or the FIA medical delegate can require a driver to have a medical examination at any time during an Event.

110. Failure to comply with the general safety requirements of the Code or these Sporting Regulations may result in the exclusion of the car and driver concerned from the Event.

FREE PRACTICE, QUALIFYING PRACTICE AND WARM UP

112. No driver may start in the race without taking part in qualifying practice.

113. During all practices there will be a green and a red light at the pit exit. Cars may only leave the pit lane when the green light is on (...)

115. Free practice sessions will take place :

a) Two days (Monaco : three days) before the race from 11.00 to 12.00 and from 13.00 to 14.00.

b) The day before the race from 09.00 to 09.45 and from 10.15 to 11.00.

116. Qualifying practice will take place :

a) The day before the race from 13.00 to 14.00.

b) Each driver is allowed a maximum of 12 laps qualifying practice. Should a driver complete more than 12 laps all times recorded by the driver will be cancelled.

117. Warm up : a free practice session will take

place on race day; it will last 30 minutes and start 4 hours and 30 minutes before the starting time of the race.

118. The interval between the free and qualifying practice session may never be less than 1 hour and 30 minutes. Only in the most exceptional circumstances can a delay in free practice or other difficulty on race morning result in a change to the starting time of the race.

119. If a car stops during practice it must be removed from the track as quickly as possible so that its presence does not constitute a danger or hinder other competitors. If the driver is unable to drive the car from a dangerous position, it shall be the duty of the marshals to assist him. If any such assistance results in the car being driven or pushed back to the pits, the car may not be used again in that session. Additionally, if the assistance is given during a pre-qualifying or qualifying practice session, the driver's fastest lap time from the relevant session will be deleted. In the event of a driving infringement during practice, the stewards may delete any number of qualifying times from the driver concerned. In this case, a Team will not be able to appeal against the steward's decision.

120. The clerk of the course may interrupt practice as often and for as long as he thinks necessary to clear the track or to allow the recovery of a car. In the case of free practice only, the clerk of the course with the agreement of the stewards may decline to prolong the practice period after an interruption of thiskind.Furthermore, if in the opinion of the stewards, a stoppage is caused deliberately, the driver concerned may have his times from that session cancelled and may not be permitted to take part in any other practice session that day.

122. Should one or more sessions be thus interrupted, no protest can be accepted as to the possible effects of the interruption on the qualification of drivers admitted to start.

123. All laps covered during qualifying practice will be timed to determine the driver's position at the start in accordance with the prescriptions of Article 129. With the exception of a lap on which a red flag is shown (see Article 155), each time a car crosses the Line it will be deemed to have completed one lap.

STOPPING THE PRACTICE

124. Should it become necessary to stop the practice because the circuit is blocked by an accident or because weather or other conditions make it dangerous to continue, the clerk of the course shall order a red flag and the abort lights to be shown at the Line. Simultaneously, red flags will be shown at all marshal posts. When the signal is given to stop, all cars shall immediately reduce speed and proceed slowly back to their respective pits, and all cars abandoned on the track will be removed to a safe place. Any lap during which the red flag is shown will not be counted towards a car's total lap allocation for that session. At the end of each practice session all drivers may cross the Line only once.

PRESS CONFERENCES AND DRIVERS PARADE

125. The FIA press delegate will choose a maximum of five drivers who must attend a press conference in the media centre for a period of one hour at 15.00 on the day before first practice. These driver's Teams will be notified no less than 48 hours before the conference. In addition, a maximum of two team personalities may be chosen by the FIA press delegate to attend this press conference. On the first day of practice, a minimum of three and a maximum of six drivers and/or team personalities, (other than those who attended the press conference on the previous day and subject to the consent of the team principal) will be chosen by ballot or rota by the FIA press delegate during the Event and must make themselves available to the media for a press conference in the media centre for a period of one hour at 15.30.

126. Immediately after qualifying practice the first three drivers in qualifying will be required to make themselves available for television interviews in the unilateral room and then attend a press conference in the media centre for a maximum period of 30 minutes.

THE GRID

128. At the end of qualifying practice, the fastest time achieved by each driver will be officially published (see Article 51).

129. The grid will be drawn up in the order of the fastest time achieved by each driver. Should two or more drivers have set identical times, priority will be given to the one who set it first.

130. The fastest driver will start the race from the position on the grid which was the pole position in the previous year or, on a new circuit, has been designated as such by the FIA safety delegate.

131. Any driver whose best qualifying lap exceeds 107% of the pole position time will not be allowed to take part in the warm up or race. Under exceptional circumstances however, which may include setting a suitable lap time in a previous free practice session, the stewards may permit the car to start the race. Should there be more than one driver accepted in this manner, their order will be determined by the stewards. In either case, a Team will not be able to appeal against the stewards' decision.

132. The starting grid will be published after the warm up on race day. Any competitor whose car(s) is (are) unable to start for any reason whatsoever (or who has good reason to believe that their car(s) will not be ready to start) must inform the clerk of the course accordingly at the earliest opportunity and, in any event, no later than 45 minutes before the start of the race. If one or more cars are withdrawn, the grid will be closed up accordingly. The final starting grid will be published 45 minutes before the start of the race.

134. Any car which has not taken up its position on the grid by the time the ten minute signal is shown, will not be permitted to do so and must start from

the pits in accordance with Article 137.

BRIEFING

135. A briefing by the race director will take place at 10.00 on the first day of practice. All drivers entered for the Event and their Team Managers must be present . Should the race director consider another briefing is necessary, it will take place one hour after the end of warm up. Competitors will be informed no later than three hours after the end of qualifying practice if this is deemed necessary.

STARTING PROCEDURE

136. 30 minutes before the time for the start of the race, the cars will leave the pits to cover a reconnaissance lap. At the end of this lap they will stop on the grid in starting order with their engines stopped. Should they wish to cover more than one reconnaissance lap, this must be done by driving down the pit lane at greatly reduced speed between each of the laps.

137. 17 minutes before the starting time, a warning signal announcing the closing of the pit exit in 2 minutes will be given. 15 minutes before the starting time, the pit exit will be closed and a second warning signal will be given. Any car which is still in the pits can start from the pits, but only under the direction of the marshals. It may be moved to the pit exit only with the driver in position. Where the pit exit is immediately after the Line, cars will join the race when the whole field has passed the pit exit on its first racing lap. Where the pit exit is immediately before the Line, cars will join the race as soon as the whole field has crossed the Line after the start.

138. Refuelling on the starting grid may only be carried out prior to the 5 minute signal and by using one unpressurised container with a maximum capacity of 12 litres. Any such container may not be refilled during the starting procedure and must be fitted with one or more dry break couplings connecting it to the car.

139. The approach of the start will be announced by signals shown ten minutes, five minutes, three minutes, one minute and thirty seconds before the start of the formation lap, each of which will be accompanied by an audible warning.

When the ten minute signal is shown, everybody except drivers, officials and team technical staff must leave the grid. When the five minute signal is shown all cars must have their wheels fitted. After this signal wheels may only be removed in the pits. Any car which does not have all its wheels fitted at the five minute signal must start the race from the back of the grid or the pit lane. When the one minute signal is shown, engines will be started and all team technical staff must leave the grid.

When the green lights are illuminated, the cars will begin the formation lap with the pole position driver leading. When leaving the grid, all drivers must proceed at a greatly reduced speed until clear of any Team personnel standing beside the track. During the formation lap practice starts are forbidden and the formation must be kept as tight as possible.

Overtaking during the formation lap is only permitted if a car is delayed when leaving its grid position and cars behind cannot avoid passing it without unduly delaying the remainder of the field. In this case, drivers may only overtake to re-establish the original starting order.

Any driver who is delayed leaving the grid may not overtake another moving car if he was stationary after the remainder of the cars had crossed the Line, and must start the race from the back of the grid. If more than one driver is affected, they must form up at the back of the grid in the order they left to complete the formation lap. If the Line is not situated in front of pole position, for the purposes of this Article only, it will be deemed to be a white line one metre in front of pole position.

A time penalty will be imposed on any driver who, in the opinion of the Stewards, unnecessarily overtook another car during the formation lap.

140. Any driver who is unable to start the formation lap must raise his arm and, after the remainder of the cars have crossed the Line, his mechanics may attempt to rectify the problem under the supervision of the marshals. If the car is still unable to start the formation lap it will be pushed into the pit lane by the shortest route and the mechanics may work on the car again.

141. When the cars come back to the grid at the end of the formation lap, they will stop on their respective grid positions, keeping their engines running. Once all the cars have come to a halt the five second signal will appear followed by the four, three, two and one second signals. At any time after the one second signal appears, the race will be started by extinguishing all red lights.

143. Any car which is unable to maintain starting order during the entire formation lap or is moving when the one second light comes on must enter the pit lane and start from the pits as specified in Article 137.

144. If, after returning to the starting grid at the end of the formation lap, a driver's engine stops and he is unable to restart the car, he must immediately raise his hands above his head and the marshal responsible for that row must immediately wave a yellow flag. If the start is delayed, (see Article 145) a marshal with a yellow flag will stand in front of the car concerned to prevent it from moving until the whole field has left the grid. The driver may then follow the procedure set out in Articles 140 and 143. As in Article 141, other cars will maintain their grid positions and the vacant position(s) will not be filled.

Should there be more than one driver in this situation, their new positions at the back of the grid will be determined in accordance with their relative positions on the grid at the start of the formation lap.

145. If a problem arises when the cars reach the starting grid at the end of the formation lap the following procedure shall apply :

a) If the race has not been started, the abort lights will be switched on, all engines will be stopped and the new formation lap will start 5 minutes later with the race distance reduced by one lap. The next signal will be the three minute signal.

b) If the race has been started the marshals alongside the grid will wave their yellow flags to inform the drivers that a car is stationary on the grid.

c) If, after the start, a car is immobilised on the starting grid, it shall be the duty of the marshals to push it into the pit lane by the fastest route. If the driver is able to re-start the car whilst it is being pushed he may rejoin the race.

d) If the driver is unable to start the car whilst it is being pushed his mechanics may attempt to start it in the pit lane. If the car then starts it may rejoin the race. The driver and mechanics must follow the instructions of the track marshals at all times during such a procedure.

147. No refuelling will be allowed on the grid if more than one start procedure proves necessary under Article 145.

148. A time penalty will be imposed for a false start judged using a FIA supplied transponder which must be fitted to the car as specified.

149. Only in the following cases will any variation in the start procedure be allowed :

a) If the track is dry throughout all practice sessions but becomes wet (or vice-versa) after the end of the warm up and at least 60 minutes before the starting time, a 15 minute free practice may be allowed.

b) If it starts to rain after the five minute signal but before the race is started and, in the opinion of the race director Teams should be given the opportunity to change tyres, the abort lights will be shown on the Line and the starting procedure will begin again at the 15 minute point. If necessary the procedure set out in Article 145 will be followed.

c) If the start of the race is imminent and, in the opinion of the race director, the volume of water on the track is such that it cannot be negotiated safely even on wet-weather tyres, the abort lights will be shown on the Line simultaneously with a "10" board with a red background. This "10" board with a red background will mean that there is to be a delay of ten minutes before the starting procedure can be resumed. If weather conditions have improved at the end of that ten minute period, a "10" board with a green background will be shown. The "10" board with a green background will mean that the green light will be shown in ten minutes. Five minutes after the "10" board with the green background is shown, the starting procedure will begin and the normal starting procedure signals (i.e. 5, 3, 1 min., 30 second) will be shown. If however, the weather conditions have not improved within ten minutes after the "10" board with the red background was shown, the abort lights will be shown on the Line and the "10" board with the red background will be shown again which will mean a further delay of ten minutes before the starting procedure can be resumed. This procedure may be repeated several times. At any time when a "10" board (with either a red or green background) is shown, it will be accompanied by an audible warning.

d) If the race is started behind the safety car, Article 154n) will apply.

THE RACE

151. A race will not be stopped in the event of rain unless the circuit is blocked or it is dangerous to continue (see Article 155).

152. If a car stops during the race (except under Article 145c and d), it must be removed from the track as quickly as possible so that its presence does not constitute a danger or hinder other competitors. If the driver is unable to drive the car from a dangerous position, it shall be the duty of the marshals to assist him. If any such assistance results in the engine starting and the driver rejoining the race, the car will be excluded from the results of the race.

153. During the race, drivers leaving the pit lane may only do so when the pit exit light is green and on their own responsibility. A marshal with a blue flag, or a flashing blue light, will also warn the driver if cars are approaching on the track.

SAFETY CAR

154 (...)b) 30 minutes before the race start time the safety car will take up position at the front of the grid and remain there until the five minute signal is given. At this point (except under n) below) it will cover a whole lap of the circuit and enter the pit lane. If Article 149a) applies, the safety car will take up its position at the front of the grid as soon as the 15 minute practice session has finished.

c) The safety car may be brought into operation to neutralise a race upon the decision of the clerk of the course. It will be used only if competitors or officials are in immediate physical danger but the circumstances are not such as to necessitate stopping the race.

d) When the order is given to deploy the safety car, all observer's posts will display immobile yellow flags and a board "SC" which shall be maintained until the intervention is over.

e) During the race, the safety car with its revolving lights on, will start from the pit lane and will join the track regardless of where the race leader is.

f) All the competing cars will form up in line behind the safety car no more than 5 car lengths apart. All overtaking is forbidden (except under n) below), unless a car is signalled to do so from the safety car.

g) When ordered to do so by the clerk of the course the observer in the car will use a green light to signal to any cars between it and the race leader that they should pass. These cars will continue at reduced speed and without overtaking until they reach the line of cars behind the safety car.

h) The safety car shall be used at least until the leader is behind it and all remaining cars are lined up behind him.(...)

i) While the safety car is in operation, competing cars may stop at their pit, but may only rejoin the track when the green light at the pit exit is on. It will be on at all times except when the safety car and the line of cars following it are about to pass or are passing the pit exit. A car rejoining the track must proceed at reduced speed until it reaches the end of the line of cars behind the safety car.

j) When the clerk of the course calls in the safety car, it must extinguish all the revolving lights, this will be the signal to the drivers that it will be entering the pit lane at the end of that lap. At this point the first car in line behind the safety car may dictate the pace and, if necessary, fall more than five car lengths behind it. As the safety car is approaching the pit entrance the yellow flags and SC boards at the observer's posts will be withdrawn and green flags will be displayed for one lap.

k) When the safety car has pulled off the circuit and the cars are approaching the Line, green lights will be shown. Overtaking remains strictly forbidden until the cars pass the green light at the Line.

l) Each lap completed while the safety car is deployed will be counted as a race lap.

m) If the race is stopped under Article 156 Case C, the safety car will take the chequered flag and all cars able to do so must follow it into the pit lane and into the parc fermé.

n) In exceptional circumstances the race may be started behind the safety car. In this case, at any time before the one minute signal, its revolving yellow lights will be turned on. This is the signal to the drivers that the race will be started behind the safety car. When the green lights are illuminated the safety car will leave the grid with all cars following in grid order no more than 5 car lengths apart. There will be no formation lap and race will start when the leading car crosses the line for the first time. Overtaking, during the first lap only, is permitted if a car is delayed when leaving its grid position and cars behind cannot avoid passing it without unduly delaying the remainder of the field. In this case, drivers may only overtake to re-establish the original starting order. Any driver who is delayed leaving the grid may not overtake another moving car if he was stationary after the remainder of the cars had crossed the Line, and must form up at the back of the line of cars behind the safety car. If more than one driver is affected, they must form up at the back of the field in the order they left the grid. A time penalty will be imposed on any driver who, in the opinion of the Stewards, unnecessarily overtook another car during the first lap.

STOPPING A RACE

155. Should it become necessary to stop the race because the circuit is blocked by an accident or because weather or other conditions make it dangerous to continue, the clerk of the course shall order a red flag and the abort lights to be shown at the Line. Simultaneously, red flags will be shown at all marshal posts. When the signal is given to stop all cars shall immediately reduce speed in the knowledge that :

- the race classification will be that at the end of the penultimate lap before the lap in which the signal to stop the race was given,

- race and service vehicles may be on the track,

- the circuit may be totally blocked because of an accident,

- weather conditions may have made the circuit undriveable at racing speed,

- the pit lane will be open.

156. The procedure to be followed varies according to the number of laps completed by the race leader before the signal to stop the race was given :

Case A : Less than two full laps. If the race can be restarted, Article 157 will apply.

Case B : Two or more full laps but less than 75% of the race distance (rounded up to the nearest whole number of laps). If the race can be restarted, Article 158 will apply.

Case C : 75% or more of the race distance (rounded up to the nearest whole number of laps). The cars will be sent directly to the parc fermé and the race will be deemed to have finished when the leading car crossed the Line for the penultimate time before the race was stopped.

RESTARTING A RACE

157. Case A.

a) The original start shall be deemed null and void.

b) The length of the restarted race will be the full original race distance.

c) The drivers who are eligible to take part in the race shall be eligible for the restart either in their original car or in a spare car.

d) After the signal to stop the race has been given, all cars able to do so will proceed directly but slowly to either :

- the pit lane or ;

- if the grid is clear. to their original grid position or ;

- if the grid is not clear, to a position behind the last grid position as directed by the marshals.

e) All cars may be worked on.

f) Refuelling will be allowed until the five minute signal is shown.

158. Case B.

a) The race shall be deemed to be in two parts, the first of which finished when the leading car crossed the Line for the penultimate time before the race was stopped.

b) The length of the second part will be three laps less than the length of the original race less the first part.

c) The grid for the second part will be a standard grid with the cars arranged in the order in which they finished the first part.

d) Only cars which took part in the original start will be eligible and then only if they returned under their own power by an authorised route to either :

- he pit lane or ;

- to a position behind the last grid position as directed by the marshals.

e) No spare car will be eligible.

f) Cars may be worked on in the pits or on the grid. If work is carried out on the grid, this must be done in the car's correct grid position and must in no way impede the re-start.

g) If a car returns to the pits it may be refuelled. If a car is refuelled it must take the re-start from the back of the grid and, if more than one car is involved, their positions will be determined by their order on the penultimate lap before the race was stopped. In this case their original grid positions will be left vacant.

159. In both Case A and Case B :

a) 10 minutes after the stop signal, the pit exit will close.

b) 15 minutes after the stop signal, the five minute signal will be shown, the grid will close and the normal start procedure will recommence.

c) Any car which is unable to take up its position on the grid before the five minute signal will be directed to the pits. It may then start from the pits as specified in Article 137. The organiser must have sufficient personnel and equipment available to enable the foregoing timetable to be adhered to even in the most difficult circumstances.

FINISH

160. The end-of-race signal will be given at the Line as soon as the leading car has covered the full race distance in accordance with Article 13. Should two hours elapse before the full distance has been covered, the end-of-race signal will be given to the leading car the first time it crosses the Line after such time has elapsed.

161. Should for any reason (other than under Article 155) the end-of-race signal be given before the leading car completes the scheduled number of laps, or the prescribed time has been completed, the race will be deemed to have finished when the leading car last crossed the Line before the signal was given. Should the end-of-race signal be delayed for any reason, the race will be deemed to have finished when it should have finished.

162. After receiving the end-of-race signal all cars must proceed on the circuit directly to the parc fermé without stopping, without receiving any object whatsoever and without any assistance (except that of the marshals if necessary). Any classified car which cannot reach the parc fermé under its own power will be placed under the exclusive control of the marshals who will take the car to the parc fermé.

PARC FERME

163. Only those officials charged with supervision may enter the parc fermé. No intervention of any kind is allowed there unless authorised by such officials.

164. When the parc fermé is in use, parc fermé regulations will apply in the area between the Line and the parc fermé entrance.

165. The parc fermé shall be sufficiently large and secure that no unauthorised persons can gain access to it.

CLASSIFICATION

166. The car placed first will be the one having covered the scheduled distance in the shortest time, or, where appropriate, passed the Line in the lead at the end of two hours. All cars will be classified taking into account the number of complete laps they have covered, and for those which have completed the same number of laps, the order in which they crossed the Line.

167. If a car takes more than twice the time of the winner's fastest lap to cover its last lap this last lap will not be taken into account when calculating the total distance covered by such car.

168. Cars having covered less than 90% of the number of laps covered by the winner (rounded down to the nearest whole number of laps), will not be classified.

169. The official classification will be published after the race. It will be the only valid result subject to any amendments which may be made under the Code and these Sporting Regulations.

PODIUM CEREMONY

170. The drivers finishing the race in 1st, 2nd and 3rd positions and a representative of the winning constructor must attend the prize-giving ceremony on the podium and abide by the podium procedure set out in Appendix 3 (except Monaco); and immediately thereafter make themselves available for a period of 90 minutes for the purpose of television unilateral interviews and the press conference in the media centre.

Meaning of the flags

White flag :	service vehicle on track
Blue flag :	(immobile) : a car is close behind you (waving) : a car is about to overtake you
Yellow flag :	(immobile) : overtaking is prohibited, danger (waving) immediate danger, slow down
Red flag :	(by marshals and the Clerk of the race) : stopping of the race on the Line
Green flag :	end of danger, free track
Yellow with red stripes flag :	danger, slippery surface
Black flag :	(with car number) : stop on the next lap
Black with yellow circle flag :	your car is in danger
Black and white flag :	non-sporting behaviour, warning
Chequered flag :	end of the race or of the practice

FORMULA ONE
TYRES BY BRIDGESTONE